P9-DEO-047

NEW DIRECTIONS FOR TEACHING AND LEARNING

Marilla D. Svinicki, *University of Texas, Austin*
EDITOR-IN-CHIEF

Motivation from Within: Approaches for Encouraging Faculty and Students to Excel

Michael Theall
University of Illinois at Springfield

EDITOR

Number 78, Summer 1999

JOSSEY-BASS PUBLISHERS
San Francisco

MOTIVATION FROM WITHIN: APPROACHES FOR ENCOURAGING FACULTY AND
STUDENTS TO EXCEL
Michael Theall (ed.)
New Directions for Teaching and Learning, no. 78
Marilla D. Svinicki, Editor-in-Chief

Copyright © 1999 Jossey-Bass Inc., Publishers, 350 Sansome Street, San
Francisco, CA 94104.

Microfilm copies of issues and articles are available in 16mm and 35mm,
as well as microfiche in 105mm, through University Microfilms Inc., 300
North Zeeb Road, Ann Arbor, Michigan 48106-1346.

ISSN 0271-0633   ISBN 0-7879-4875-6

NEW DIRECTIONS FOR TEACHING AND LEARNING is part of The Jossey-Bass
Higher and Adult Education Series and is published quarterly by Jossey-
Bass Inc., Publishers, 350 Sansome Street, San Francisco, California
94104-1342. Periodicals postage paid at San Francisco, California, and at
additional mailing offices. Postmaster: Send address changes to New
Directions for Teaching and Learning, Jossey-Bass Inc., Publishers, 350
Sansome Street, San Francisco, California 94104-1342.

New Directions for Teaching and Learning is indexed in College Student
Personnel Abstracts, Contents Pages in Education, and Current Index to
Journals in Education (ERIC).

SUBSCRIPTIONS cost $56.00 for individuals and $99.00 for institutions,
agencies, and libraries. Prices subject to change.

EDITORIAL CORRESPONDENCE should be sent to the editor-in-chief, Marilla
D. Svinicki, The Center for Teaching Effectiveness, University of Texas at
Austin, Main Building 2200, Austin, TX 78712-1111.

Cover photograph by Richard Blair/Color & Light © 1990.

www.josseybass.com

Printed in the United States of America on acid-free recycled paper containing 100 percent recovered waste paper, of which at least 20 percent is
postconsumer waste.

CONTENTS

About This Publication. Since 1980, *New Directions for Teaching and Learning* (NDTL) has brought a unique blend of theory, research, and practice to leaders in postsecondary education. NDTL sourcebooks strive not only for solid substance but also for timeliness, compactness, and accessibility.

The series has four goals: to inform readers about current and future directions in teaching and learning in postsecondary education, to illuminate the context that shapes these new directions, to illustrate these new directions through examples from real settings, and to propose ways in which these new directions can be incorporated into still other settings.

This publication reflects our view that teaching deserves respect as a high form of scholarship. We believe that significant scholarship is conducted not only by researchers who report results of empirical investigations but also by practitioners who share disciplined reflections about teaching. Contributors to NDTL approach questions of teaching and learning as seriously as they approach substantive questions in their own disciplines, and they deal not only with pedagogical issues but also with the intellectual and social context in which these issues arise. Authors deal on the one hand with theory and research and on the other with practice, and they translate from research and theory to practice and back again.

About This Volume. In the current issue the authors illustrate the broad range of ways that the topic of motivation can be applied to higher education. Motivation can be thought of from the perspective of the students, of the instructor, and of the institution itself. The chapters provide a solid foundation in theory and research to illuminate practices that can enhance motivation for all the interacting groups.

MARILLA D. SVINICKI, *editor-in-chief, is director of the Center for Teaching Effectiveness at the University of Texas, Austin.*

EDITOR'S NOTES

The topic of motivation is a broad one. An extensive literature on motivation exists and touches on so many other aspects of behavior and learning that no one book could hope to cover the breadth of the field. For that reason, the focus of this issue of *New Directions for Teaching and Learning* is on motivation in higher education and on the common elements that can be found when motivation is discussed with respect to instructional process and the university community—that is, with respect to teachers, learners, administrators, and staff. Although the authors of this issue recognize and refer to many of the classic works in the field, much of what is reported here is new: new studies, new syntheses, and explorations of new situations. In every chapter attention is given to the application of motivational theories and principles to specific situations, and to the importance of incorporating motivational concepts into everyday pedagogical or administrative practice.

The most common thread running through the chapters is that motivation is a construct that describes how individuals respond to sets of conditions in light of their own perspectives, attitudes, and beliefs. Individuals choose to do or not do certain things, and in this sense the authors of this issue focus on factors, situations, or strategies that keep individual differences in mind and that accommodate these differences.

We often think of *intrinsic* and *extrinsic* motivation as defined by the locus of the reward, but here our view is that motivation is not something one "does to" someone else. While it is true, for example, that tangible rewards such as financial incentives are external to the individual, the decision to pursue these rewards must come from within. The implication of this approach is that our efforts to "motivate" teachers, learners, or others, should target their values, needs, and orientations, that an understanding of the individual allows teachers or others to provide sets of conditions that will prompt positive intrinsic motivation. In other words, our task is to create situations in which others provide their own motivation to succeed. This approach does not suggest that teachers, administrators, or other leaders abdicate their responsibility to define, to set direction, to establish standards and criteria, or to assess and evaluate performance. On the contrary, good motivational practice requires careful delineation of the parameters of learning or working situations as well as of the goals that must be achieved. The thrust here is to engage others in a common quest by involving them in decision making, assisting them with resources and guidance for task completion, monitoring their progress, and trusting them to assume responsible leadership roles. We hope that this issue will provide some useful guidelines for teachers, learners, and administrators who wish to maximize their own performance and at the same time help others to do the same.

The issue has four parts. In Part One we consider motivation and learners. We begin with Raymond J. Wlodkowski's discussion of motivation (which he defines as "the natural human capacity to direct energy in the pursuit of a goal") as a diverse construct that includes the crucial notion that helping a person to learn requires "understanding a person's thinking and emotions as inseparable from the social context in which the [learning] activity takes place." This chapter establishes a perspective for the rest of the issue, placing the definition of *intrinsic motivation* at the forefront and stressing the importance of individual differences, particularly those that are culturally based. Wlodkowski proceeds to describe a motivational framework for responsive teaching.

In Chapter Two, Michael B. Paulsen and Kenneth A. Feldman, and in Chapter Three, Janet G. Donald, discuss student belief systems, first with respect to the organization and structure of students' beliefs about knowledge, and then with respect to the higher-order learning that is supposed to be the hallmark of higher education. These new investigations shed light on some of the problems faced by learners as they struggle with subject material at different levels of difficulty, and by teachers as they attempt to share successfully the depth of their understanding and the breadth of their disciplines. The authors provide suggestion for better research, better practice, and better learning.

In Part Two, motivation is considered as part of instructional processes or methods. These chapters provide concrete examples of the application of motivational theory and research to specific teaching and learning situations and techniques.

First, in Chapter Four, John M. Keller deals with the application of his ARCS (attention, relevance, confidence, and satisfaction) instructional motivation model in settings with two unusual aspects: international locations and technological applications (computer-based instruction and distance education formats). Keller describes the applicability of the model and the results of its use. He is followed in Chapter Five by Marjorie M. MacKinnon, who reports on the use of *problem-based learning,* also in an international setting. MacKinnon focuses on qualitative data found in student journals and relates her findings to motivational research. Next, in Chapter Six, Theodore Panitz presents a synthesis of research and practice related to the motivational underpinnings of cooperative learning. He describes a net of motivational constructs that make cooperative learning effective, thus providing teachers with many options for course design.

Part Three considers the institutional perspective, discussing the motivational aspects of supporting teaching, programs, and change efforts across the institution. In Chapter Seven, Kenneth A. Feldman and Michael B. Paulsen discuss *teaching cultures* and the characteristics of these cultures related to success in improving instructional quality. They review faculty motivations to teach and what can be done to support faculty in their efforts to improve. Edward B. Nuhfer follows in Chapter Eight with a discussion of motivation in institutional interdisciplinary programs. He offers considerations for teachers, learners, administrators, and often-forgotten staff of units whose functions are critical to successful interdisciplinary efforts. This chapter begins to bring a broader view of motivation as an issue that goes beyond the classroom and into all aspects of higher education.

Chapter Nine, by Donald W. Farmer, on motivating faculty for institutional improvement, is based on the author's extensive experience as a teacher and administrator at an institution that has, over the past fifteen years, been involved in a comprehensive assessment effort. Farmer discusses the array of stakeholders in an institutional improvement program and offers suggestions for all participants, from academic vice presidents to faculty to staff. Proactive leadership and commitment at several levels within the institution are the key to success in major innovative change efforts.

In Part Four, the concluding chapter by Jennifer Franklin and me extracts guidelines from the issue and offers a general model for motivation in higher education. It attempts to bring together those concepts, strategies, and considerations that are most generalizable and applicable to the range of higher education activities, with a concentration on the underlying mission of higher education: teaching and learning.

Michael Theall
Editor

MICHAEL THEALL is associate professor of educational administration and director of the Center for Teaching and Learning at the University of Illinois at Springfield.

PART ONE

Motivation and Learners

Motivation is the natural human capacity to direct energy in the pursuit of a goal, and learning is a naturally active and normally volitional process, but that process cannot be separated from the cultural context of the classroom or from the background of the learner.

Motivation and Diversity: A Framework for Teaching

Raymond J. Wlodkowski

Historically, motivation and sex share a similar fate: both promise extraordinary rewards but when actually realized they continue to mystify and confuse. At the core of each is desire. Yet maintaining a passion for learning or for another person can fall prey to distraction as well as to other interests. What seemed to be a dream that would last forever may quickly disappear because of something as banal as familiarity or monotony.

One of the problems with understanding motivation is that we cannot see it and we cannot touch it. It is what is known in the social sciences as a hypothetical construct, an invented definition that provides a possible concrete causal explanation of behavior. Therefore we cannot observe motivation directly nor measure it precisely. We have to infer it from what people do. So we look for signs such as persistence and completion.

We also know that culture—that deeply learned mix of language, beliefs, values, and behaviors that pervades every aspect of our lives—significantly influences our motivation. In fact, social scientists today regard the cognitive processes as inherently cultural (Rogoff and Chavajay, 1995). The language we use to think and the ways in which we communicate cannot be separated from cultural practices and cultural context. As Vivian Gussin Paley (1990, p. xii) writes, "None of us are to be found in sets of tasks or lists of attributes; we can be known only in the unfolding of our unique stories within the context of everyday events."

This chapter is concerned with motivation to learn and how to encourage it effectively. Learning is a naturally active and normally volitional process of constructing meaning from information and experience (Lambert and McCombs, 1998). Motivation is the natural human capacity to direct energy in the pursuit of a goal. Although our lives are marked by a continuous flow of activity within an infinite variety of overt actions, we are purposeful. We constantly learn, and when we do we are usually motivated to learn. We are directing our energy through the processes of attention, concentration, and imagination, to name only few, to make sense of our world.

Until about a decade ago, an individualistic understanding of motivation dominated the field of psychology. Personal motives, thoughts, expectancies, and goals were concepts that had a strong influence on psychological approaches to facilitating student motivation and learning. Currently, *socioconstructivism* is a rapidly growing theoretical force in understanding ways to improve learning in schools and colleges (Hickey, 1997). Critical to this view is the realization that people learn through their interaction with and support from other people and objects in the world. We are more aware that to help a person learn may require understanding his or her thinking and emotions as inseparable from the social context in which the activity takes place.

In terms of the current state of research and practice, it seems wise to allow both individualistic and socio-constructivist theories to inform how we teach (Salomon and Perkins, 1998). For example, there is little doubt that what a student finds personally relevant is a socially constructed meaning—that is, it is based on social experience and values. However, to find, edit, and organize an essay based on personally relevant material takes considerable individual reflection and self-direction. This kind of self-regulation is largely an individual process and we benefit from understanding the considerable research that describes how to teach students these skills (Pintrich, 1995).

Because of the rich cultural diversity within this country, we need models to guide teachers in effective ways to access and strengthen their students' individual skills as well as ways to include the understanding they bring to learning based on their social experiences. The Motivational Framework for Culturally Responsive Teaching (Wlodkowski and Ginsberg, 1995) is a model for teaching and for planning instruction based on the principle that individual motivation is inseparable from culture. It offers a pedagogical approach for creating learning experiences that evoke the intrinsic motivation of all students.

After a discussion of motivation and culture, this chapter proceeds to explore some important differences between intrinsic and extrinsic motivation. It continues with an overview of the motivational framework and ends with how to plan lessons to elicit intrinsic motivation among culturally diverse students.

Motivation: Inseparable from Culture

Colleges have increasing numbers of culturally diverse students. To be effective with all students, faculty have to relate their content to their students' experiences and the ways in which their students know. Teaching that ignores student norms of behavior and communication provokes student resistance, while teaching that is responsive prompts student involvement (Olneck, 1995).

Engagement in learning is the visible outcome of motivation. Our emotions are a part of and significantly influence our motivation. In turn, our emotions are socialized through culture. For example, one person working at a task feels frustrated and stops while another person working at the task feels joy and continues. Yet another person with an even different set of cultural beliefs feels frustrated at the task but continues with increased determination. What may elicit that frustration, joy, or determination may differ across cultures, because cultures differ in their definitions of novelty, hazard, opportunity, and gratification, and in their definitions of appropriate responses (Kitayama and Markus, 1994).

Today teachers inevitably face the reality that what may enhance the motivation of some students may diminish the motivation of others. Icebreakers are a good example of this phenomenon. Many courses begin with activities to create a more sociable mood. Some of these activities ask students to self-disclose intimate personal feelings or circumstances to other students, who at the time are strangers to them. Some students enjoy sharing such personal information with people who are relatively unknown to them. Studies consistently reveal, however, that self-disclosure of this nature may be incompatible with the cultural values of Asian Americans, Latinos, and American Indians, who often reserve expression of very personal feelings for the intimacy of family (Sue and Sue, 1990). An early request for such self-disclosure might be disconcerting for students from these ethnic backgrounds and stimulate a sense of alienation from the rest of the class or from the course itself. Without sensitivity to culture, we teachers may unknowingly contribute to the decline of motivation among our students.

Extrinsic and Intrinsic Motivation: Important Social Differences

Although the cognitive revolution is more than thirty years old, most colleges are locked in midcentury with a deterministic, mechanistic, and behavioristic orientation toward student motivation. Using a system of competitive evaluation procedures, grades, and grade point averages, with the "carrot" being eligibility for select vocations and graduate schools, they follow the precepts of extrinsic reinforcement. With few exceptions, postsecondary education is a system based on the assumption that human beings will strive to learn when they are externally rewarded for learning or punished for lack of it. Those students whose socialization accommodates this extrinsic approach tend to succeed, while those students—often the culturally different—whose socialization does not accommodate it fall behind. Colleges successfully educate a disproportionately low number of low-income and ethnic minority students (Wlodkowski and Ginsberg, 1995). Because the importance of grades and grade point averages increases as a student advances in college, it is legitimate to question whether extrinsic motivation systems are effective for significant numbers of students across cultures.

Although there has been debate among psychologists about the merits of extrinsic reward systems (Cameron and Pierce, 1996), the general principles of the American Psychological Association's Task Force on Psychology in Education (Lambert and McCombs, 1998) clearly support an intrinsic motivation system for learning among all students. The goal of the research was to determine how psychological knowledge synthesized from studies throughout the twentieth century could contribute directly to improvement in student achievement and the design of educational systems. Lambert and McCombs (1998) concluded that it is part of human nature to be curious, to be active, to initiate thought and behavior, to make meaning from experience, and to be effective at what we value. These primary sources of motivation reside in all of us, across all cultures. When students can see that what they are learning is important, their motivation emerges.

In learning, intrinsic motivation occurs when the activity and milieu of learning elicit motivation in the student. In extrinsic motivation systems, teachers are perceived to motivate students through the engineering of rewards and punishments. In intrinsic systems, teachers and students create opportunities, experiences, or environments that are likely to evoke motivation. This difference in the perceived source of motivation is extremely important for reasons of respect and social equity. The prevailing question in an extrinsic system of motivation is, How do I motivate them? This question might imply that less motivated students are somehow dependent, less capable of self-motivation, and in need of help from a more powerful other. At minimum, it suggests that motivation can somehow be imposed on others. Such a view is likely to heighten a teacher's perception of reluctant students as motivationally dysfunctional, to increase the tendency not to trust the perspectives of those students, and to avoid student-centered approaches to teaching and learning. In an intrinsic system of motivation it is essential to rely on the student's perspective and to hear the student's voice. This reciprocity between the teacher and the student helps us as teachers to realize the importance of cultural relevance in instruction. It also helps us to be aware that the responsibility for learner motivation lies not only within the student but also within the institution and within the structure of our courses.

The Motivational Framework
for Culturally Responsive Teaching

To promote equitable learning opportunities for all students, a holistic, culturally responsive pedagogy based on intrinsic motivation is needed. The Motivational Framework for Culturally Responsive Teaching (Wlodkowski and Ginsberg, 1995) is respectful of different cultures and is capable of creating a common culture within a learning situation that all students can accept. It dynamically combines the essential motivational conditions that are intrinsically motivating for diverse students (see Figure 1.1). Motivational strategies from an individualistic or socio-constructivist perspective can be assigned and

Figure 1.1. A Motivational Framework
for Culturally Responsive Teaching

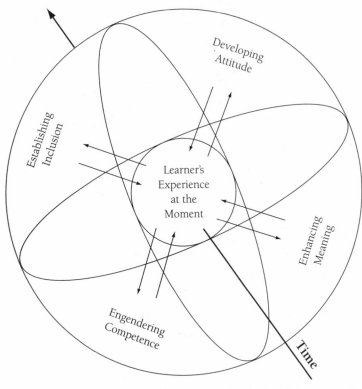

Source: Wlodkowski and Ginsberg, 1995, p. 29. Used by permission of Jossey-Bass Inc., Publishers.

understood according to the condition to which they most obviously contribute. Each of these major conditions is research-based across a number of
disciplines (Wlodkowski, 1998).

The Motivational Framework for Culturally Responsive Teaching system-
ically represents four intersecting motivational conditions that teachers and
students can create or enhance:

Establishing inclusion: Creating a learning atmosphere in which students and
   teachers feel respected and connected to one another
Developing attitude: Creating a favorable disposition toward the learning experience through personal relevance and choice
Enhancing meaning: Creating challenging, thoughtful learning experiences that
   include students' perspectives and values
Engendering competence: Creating an understanding that students are effective
   in learning something they value

As discussed earlier, researchers increasingly view cognition as a social activity that integrates the mind, the body, the process of the activity, and the ingredients of the setting in a complex interactive manner (Lave, 1988). The conventional psychological model of perceiving, thinking, and acting is a linear process that may occur far less often than previous theorists have imagined. Because the four motivational conditions work in concert and exert their influence on student learning in the moment as well as over time, the teacher is wise to plan how to establish and coordinate these conditions where possible.

Motivational planning should be integrated with instructional planning (Wlodkowski, 1998). This will help to avoid a serious pitfall common in teaching: blaming the students for being unresponsive to instruction. With no motivational plan, especially with students who are culturally different from ourselves, we are more likely to place responsibility for this lack of responsiveness on the students. It is difficult for us to be openly self-critical. Defense mechanisms such as rationalization and projection act to protect our egos. Motivational planning helps us to keep our attention on the learning climate, on how we instruct, and on what we can do about that instruction when it is not as vital as we would like it to be. This diminishes our tendency to blame, which is a common reaction to problems that seem unsolvable.

Applying the Motivational Framework for Culturally Responsive Teaching

Let us take a look at the Motivational Framework for Culturally Responsive Teaching in terms of the teaching and learning process. Because most instructional plans have specific learning objectives, they tend to be linear and prescriptive: teachers sequence learning events over time and predetermine the order in which concepts and skills will be taught and when they will be practiced and applied. Although human motivation does not always follow an orderly path, we can plan ways to evoke it throughout a learning sequence. In fact, due to motivation's emotional base and natural instability, it is judicious, especially when facing a time-limited learning period, to painstakingly plan the milieu and learning activities to enhance student motivation. For projects, self-directed learning, and situational learning, as in the case of problem posing, we may not be so bound to a formal plan.

The most basic way to begin is for the teacher to take the four motivational conditions from the framework and transpose them into questions to use as guidelines for selecting motivational strategies (Wlodkowski, 1998) and related learning activities to include in the design of the instructional plan. For example,

Establishing inclusion: How do we create or affirm a learning atmosphere in which we feel respected by and connected to one another? (best to plan for the *beginning* of the lesson)

Developing attitude: How do we create or affirm a favorable disposition toward learning through personal relevance and choice? (best to plan for the *beginning* of the lesson)

Enhancing meaning: How do we create engaging and challenging learning experiences that include students' perspectives and values? (best to plan *throughout* the lesson)

Engendering competence: How do we create or affirm an understanding that students have effectively learned something they value and perceive as authentic to their real world? (best to plan for the *end* of the lesson)

Let us look at an actual episode of teaching in which a teacher uses the motivational framework and these questions to compose an instructional plan. In this example the teacher is conducting the first two-hour session of an introductory course in research. There are twenty students ranging in age from nineteen to fifty-five. Some hold full-time jobs. Most are women. Most are first-generation college students. A few are students of color. The instructor knows from previous experience that many of these students view research as abstract, irrelevant, and oppressive learning. Her instructional objective is as follows: *Students will devise an in-class investigation and develop their own positive perspectives toward active research.* Using the motivational conditions and their related questions, the instructor creates the sequence of learning activities found in Table 1.1.

The narrative for this teaching episode goes like this: The teacher explains that much research is conducted on a collaborative basis. The course will model this approach as well. For a beginning activity she randomly assigns learners to small groups and encourages them to discuss any previous experiences they may have had doing research and their expectations and concerns for the course (strategy: collaborative learning). Each group then shares its experiences, expectations, and concerns as the teacher records them on the overhead projector. In this manner she is able to understand her students' perspectives and increase their connection to one another and herself (motivational condition: establishing inclusion).

The teacher explains that most people are researchers much of the time. She asks the students what they would like to research among themselves (strategy: relevant learning goal). After a lively discussion, the class decides to investigate and predict the amount of sleep some members of the class had the previous night. This strategy engages student choice, increases the relevance of the activity, and contributes to a favorable disposition emerging in the course (motivational condition: developing attitude). The students are learning in a way that includes their experiences and perspectives.

Five students volunteer to serve as subjects and the other students form research teams. Each team develops a set of observations and a set of questions to ask the volunteers, but no one may ask them how many hours of sleep they had the night before. After they ask their questions, the teams rank the five volunteers from the most to the least amount of sleep (strategy: critical questioning

Table 1.1. An Instructional Plan Based on the Four Questions from the Motivational Framework for Culturally Responsive Teaching

Motivational Condition and Question	Motivational Strategy	Learning Activity
Establishing inclusion: How do we create or affirm a learning atmosphere in which we feel respected by and connected to one another? (beginning)	Collaborative learning	Randomly form small groups in which students exchange experiences and expectations they have about research. List them.
Developing attitude: How do we create or affirm a favorable disposition toward learning through personal relevance and choice? (beginning)	Relevant learning goals	Ask students to choose something they want to research immediately among themselves.
Enhancing meaning: How do we create engaging and challenging learning experiences that include students' perspectives and values? (throughout)	Critical questioning and predicting	Form research teams to devise a set of questions to ask in order to make predictions. Record questions and predictions.
Engendering competence: How do we create or affirm an understanding that students have effectively learned something they value and perceive as authentic to their real world? (ending)	Self-assessment	After the predictions have been verified, ask students to create their own statements about what they learned about research from this process.

and predicting). When the volunteers reveal the amount of time they slept, the students discover that no research team was correct in ranking more than three volunteers. The students discuss why this outcome may have occurred and consider questions that might have increased their accuracy, such as, "How much coffee did you drink before you came to class?" The questioning, testing of ideas, and predicting heighten the engagement, challenge, and complexity of this learning for the students (motivational condition: enhancing meaning).

After the discussion, the teacher asks the students to write a series of statements about what this activity has taught them about research (strategy: self-assessment). Students then break into small groups to exchange their insights. Their comments include statements such as, "Research is more a method than an answer" and "Thus far I enjoy research more than I thought I would." Self-assessment helps the students to extract from this experience a new understanding that they value (motivational condition: engendering competence).

This snapshot of teaching illustrates how the four motivational conditions constantly influence and interact with one another. Without establishing inclusion (small groups to discuss concerns and experiences) and developing attitude (student choosing a relevant research goal), the enhancement of meaning (research teams devising questions and predictions) may not have occurred with ease and energy, and the self-assessment to engender competence (what students learned, from their perspective) may have had a dismal outcome. Overall the total learning experience encourages equitable participation, provides the beginning of an inclusive history for the students, and enhances their learning about research.

This class session, like all learning experiences, was systemic. It can be imagined that removing any one of the four motivational conditions would have affected the entire experience and each condition's link to the entire course. For example, would the students' attitudes have been as positive if the teacher had arbitrarily given them the task to research sleep among themselves? Probably not.

One of the values of the Motivational Framework for Culturally Responsive Teaching is that it is not only a model of motivation in action but also an organizational aid for designing instruction. By continually attending to the framework's four motivational conditions and their related questions, the teacher can select motivational strategies from a wide array of theories and literature to apply throughout a learning unit (Wlodkowski, 1998).

For using this framework, *pedagogical alignment*—the coordination of approaches to teaching that ensures maximum consistent effect—is critical (Wlodkowski, 1997). The more harmonious the elements of the instructional design are, the more likely it is that they will sustain intrinsic motivation. That is why one strategy alone, such as cooperative learning or self-assessment, is unlikely to evoke intrinsic motivation. It is the mutual influence of a combination of strategies chosen on the basis of motivational conditions that elicits intrinsic motivation.

This framework provides a holistic design that includes a time orientation, cultural perspectives, and a logical method to foster intrinsic motivation among students from the beginning to the end of an instructional unit. The purpose of the model is to respectfully evoke, support, and enhance the motivation to learn that all students possess by virtue of their humanity, and to make the teacher a valuable resource and vital partner in their realization of successful learning.

References

Cameron, J., and Pierce, W. D. "The Debate About Rewards and Intrinsic Motivation: Protests and Accusations Do Not Alter the Results." *Review of Educational Research,* 1996, 66, 39–51.

Hickey, D. T. "Motivation and Contemporary Socio-Constructivist Instructional Perspectives." *Educational Psychologist,* 1997, 32 (3), 175–193.

Kitayama, S., and Markus, H. R. (eds.). "Emotion and Culture: Empirical Studies of Mutual Influence." Washington, D.C.: American Psychological Association, 1994.

Lambert, N. M., and McCombs, B. L. "Introduction: Learner-Centered Schools and Classrooms as a Direction for School Reform." In N. M. Lambert and B. L. McCombs (eds.), *How Students Learn: Reforming Schools Through Learner-Centered Education.* Washington, D.C.: American Psychological Association, 1998.

Lave, J. "Cognition and Practice." Cambridge, England: Cambridge University Press, 1988.

Olneck, M. R. "Immigrants and Education." In J. A. Banks and C.A.M. Banks (eds.), *Handbook of Research on Multicultural Education*. New York: Macmillan, 1995.

Paley, V. G. *The Boy Who Would Be a Helicopter: The Uses of Storytelling in the Classroom*. Cambridge, Mass.: Harvard University Press, 1990.

Pintrich, P. R. (ed.). *Understanding Self-Regulated Learning*. New Directions for Teaching and Learning, no. 63. San Francisco: Jossey-Bass, 1995.

Rogoff, B., and Chavajay, P. "What's Become of Research on the Cultural Basis of Cognitive Development?" *American Psychologist*, 1995, *50*, 859–877.

Salomon, G., and Perkins, D. N. "Individual and Social Aspects of Learning." *Review of Research in Education*, 1998, *23*, 1–24.

Sue, D. W., and Sue, D. *Counseling the Culturally Different: Theory and Practice*. (2nd ed.) New York: Wiley, 1990.

Wlodkowski, R. J. "Motivation with a Mission: Understanding Motivation and Culture in Workshop Design." In J. A. Fleming (ed.), *New Perspectives on Designing and Implementing Effective Workshops*. New Directions for Adult and Continuing Education, no. 76. San Francisco: Jossey-Bass, 1997.

Wlodkowski, R. J. *Enhancing Adult Motivation to Learn: A Comprehensive Guide for Teaching All Adults*. (Rev. ed.) San Francisco: Jossey-Bass, 1998.

Wlodkowski, R. J., and Ginsberg, M. E. *Diversity and Motivation: Culturally Responsive Teaching*. San Francisco: Jossey-Bass, 1995.

RAYMOND J. WLODKOWSKI is research professor at the School for Professional Studies at Regis University, Denver, Colorado.

The motivation of students to learn is related to their epistemological beliefs. Faculty can promote student motivation by designing learning activities that facilitate student development of more sophisticated epistemological beliefs.

Student Motivation and Epistemological Beliefs

Michael B. Paulsen, Kenneth A. Feldman

College professors face the persistent challenge of encouraging their students to become well motivated and actively engaged learners. Research has consistently demonstrated that the motivational beliefs of college students have direct effects on their academic performance. These beliefs also have indirect effects because of their intermediate influence on students' use of learning and self-regulatory strategies, which in turn affect academic performance (Paulsen and Gentry, 1995; Pintrich and Schrauben, 1992). Research has also indicated that the epistemological beliefs of students—that is, their beliefs about the nature of knowledge and learning—affect their motivational beliefs, cognitive strategies, and learning outcomes (Bruning, Schraw, and Ronning, 1995; Hofer and Pintrich, 1997; Schommer, 1990). More specifically, two exploratory studies have indicated that the nature and sophistication of students' epistemological beliefs are significantly related to students' motivation to learn (Hofer, 1994; Schutz, Pintrich, and Young, 1993). However, these exploratory studies have been based on unidimensional and discipline-specific measures of epistemological beliefs and have examined their relationships with only a small range of motivational constructs. In this chapter we examine some empirical relationships we found between more comprehensive, multidimensional measures of both motivational and epistemological beliefs. Moreover, we provide practical recommendations to help faculty promote their students' motivation to learn by designing learning activities that facilitate their students' development of more sophisticated and motivationally productive epistemological beliefs.

Understanding and Measuring Students' Motivation to Learn

Motivation can be defined as the factors and processes that initiate and direct the magnitude, persistence, and quality of goal-directed behaviors (Dweck and Elliott, 1983). One theory of motivation that is particularly useful for combining the contributions of multiple models for explaining achievement behavior is expectancy-value theory (Keller, 1983; Pintrich and Schunk, 1996). When applied to people in educational settings, this theory asserts that students will engage in academic tasks when they perceive them to be of personal value and expect themselves to be successful in task performance.

Value and Motivation. McKeachie and colleagues (1990) and Pintrich (1989) conceptualize the process that students employ when attaching value to an academic task in terms of two components: goal orientation and task value. Such value assessments reflect students' reasons for engaging in a classroom activity and their individual answers to the question, "Why am I doing this task?" (Pintrich, 1989, p. 120). Studies of college student learning typically indicate that an intrinsic goal orientation tends to enhance a student's academic performance and an extrinsic goal orientation tends to constrain one's performance. Some adaptive learners, however, can figure out how to balance both types of orientations (Dweck and Leggett, 1988; Paulsen and Gentry, 1995; Pintrich and Garcia, 1991).

Students attach values to specific academic tasks that are dependent on both personal and task characteristics (Eccles, 1983). Schiefele's (1991) conception of task-specific interest is operationalized in terms of whether a student is interested or indifferent, and whether the task seems meaningful or unimportant, useful or worthless. Research consistently indicates that the values students associate with academic tasks are directly related to their task-related academic performance (Paulsen and Gentry, 1995; Pintrich, 1989; Pintrich and Garcia, 1991).

Expectancy and Motivation. *Expectancy* refers to students' beliefs about the likelihood that they will perform well on particular academic tasks (Keller, 1983; McKeachie and others, 1990). The expectations held by students regarding their performance on academic tasks are related to their beliefs about the degree of self-efficacy and internal control they have with respect to various features of task-related performance. Such beliefs determine how students would respond to the question, "Can I do this task?" (Pintrich, 1989, p. 123).

Studies of college student learning consistently indicate that both self-efficacy—seeing oneself as being able to organize and implement specific actions required for successful performance of particular academic tasks (Bandura, 1977)—and beliefs about control of learning—students' perceptions that they can influence academic outcomes through their own actions, such as increasing their effort when studying (Lefcourt, 1982)—are directly related to academic performance (Findley and Cooper, 1983; Paulsen and Gentry, 1995; Pintrich and Garcia, 1991).

Affect and Motivation. *Affective behavior* refers to the emotional aspects of students' responses to their academic task-related experiences. Such responses are reflected in students' answers to the question, "How do I feel about this task?" (Pintrich, 1989, p. 4) and are related to students' processing of information. Test anxiety is a widely used indicator of the emotional responses that illustrate affective aspects of motivation in the performance of academic tasks. Studies of college student learning indicate that test anxiety is often inversely related to academic performance (Benjamin, McKeachie, and Lin, 1987; Pintrich and Garcia, 1991).

Motivation and Its Measurement. In the present study, we used the Motivated Strategies for Learning Questionnaire (MSLQ) (Pintrich, Smith, Garcia, and McKeachie, 1991, 1993) to measure each of the motivational constructs just discussed. The MSLQ is one of the most widely used and well-known instruments available for examining the multidimensional construct of motivation to learn. It has separate scales for the assessment of each of the six motivational constructs previously discussed. These scales—intrinsic goal orientation, extrinsic goal orientation, task value, control of learning, self-efficacy, and test anxiety—constitute a questionnaire with thirty-one items.

Understanding and Measuring Students' Epistemological Beliefs

Epistemological beliefs may be defined as systems of personal and often implicit beliefs or assumptions that students hold about the nature of knowledge and learning (Hofer and Pintrich, 1997; Schommer, 1990). Most research on epistemological beliefs has focused on the intellectual development of students during the college years, and such research has emphasized students' advancement through stages, phases, or positions corresponding to progressively more mature or sophisticated epistemological beliefs (Belenky, Clinchy, Goldberger, and Tarule, 1986; Perry, 1970).

The Reconceptualization of Epistemological Beliefs. Observing that studies of the relationship between one-dimensional measures of epistemological beliefs and students' learning had led to inconsistent findings (Ryan, 1984), Schommer (1990) hypothesized that the complexity of epistemological beliefs was not adequately captured by existing measures. She proposed a multidimensional construct that viewed epistemological beliefs as a system of relatively independent beliefs about both the nature of knowledge and the nature of learning. She addressed beliefs about the nature of knowledge (simple or complex, absolute or tentative) and the source of knowledge (originating more from authority or more from reason) (Schommer, 1990, 1994a). She then supplemented the nature-of-knowledge dimensions with two beliefs about the nature of learning. The first of these beliefs views the speed of learning as either quick or gradual, and the second views one's ability to learn as either something that is fixed or something that can be improved over time. Four dimensions of epistemological beliefs resulted: two beliefs about the nature of knowledge (structure and certainty) and two beliefs about the nature of learning (speed and control).

Epistemological Beliefs and Their Measurement. In the present study, we used the Epistemological Beliefs Questionnaire (EBQ) (Schommer, 1990) to measure each of the four dimensions that constitute the construct of epistemological beliefs just discussed. This sixty-three-item questionnaire is one of the most widely used instruments available for examining epistemological beliefs as multidimensional constructs, and it has frequently been used in the study of such beliefs among college students (Paulsen and Wells, 1998; Schommer, 1993). Higher values on each of the four scales of the EBQ indicate more naive beliefs, while lower values indicate more sophisticated beliefs. Scores on the *simple knowledge* scale range from beliefs that "knowledge is organized as isolated bits and pieces" to beliefs that "knowledge is organized as highly interwoven concepts"; scores on the *certain knowledge* scale range from beliefs that "knowledge is absolute" to beliefs that "knowledge is tentative"; *fixed ability* scores range from beliefs that "the ability to learn is fixed at birth" to beliefs that "the ability to learn can be changed"; and scores on the *quick learning* scale range from beliefs that "knowledge is acquired quickly or not at all" to beliefs that "knowledge is acquired gradually" (Schommer 1994a, p. 28).

Our sample consisted of 246 students attending a large urban public university. These students were enrolled in four sections of the same course, "Introduction to the Study of Education" (required of all education majors).

Results of the Correlational Analysis

Pearson correlation coefficients and their levels of significance are reported in Table 2.1 for each possible pairing of one of the six motivational constructs and one of the four dimensions of epistemological beliefs. Because of the relatively small sample size (n = 246), in addition to correlations significant at the traditional levels of .01 and .05, correlations significant at the level of .1 are also reported for heuristic purposes.

Three of the four dimensions of epistemological beliefs were found to be significantly related to four or more of the motivational constructs. More specifically, fourteen out of twenty-four possible correlations between epistemological beliefs and motivation to learn were found to be statistically significant. Compared to students with the sophisticated belief that the structure of knowledge is complex, students with the naive belief that the structure of knowledge is simple were less likely to have an intrinsic goal orientation, to appreciate the value of learning tasks, to perceive an internal control over learning, and to feel efficacious about their capacity to learn. Students with the naive belief in simple knowledge were also more likely to have an extrinsic goal orientation and to experience higher levels of test anxiety than were students with more sophisticated beliefs.

Students with the naive belief that learning takes place quickly, compared to students with the more sophisticated belief that learning takes place gradu-

Table 2.1. Correlations Between Motivational Constructs and Epistemological Beliefs

Motivational Constructs	Dimensions of Epistemological Belief			
	Simple Knowledge	Certain Knowledge	Quick Learning	Fixed Ability
Intrinsic Goal Orientation	−.39***	+.01	−.13**	−.28***
Extrinsic Goal Orientation	+.28***	−.02	+.12*	−.03
Task Value	−.12*	+.04	−.14**	−.34***
Control of Learning	−.24***	−.07	−.12*	−.33***
Self-Efficacy	−.30***	−.06	−.05	−.31***
Test Anxiety	+.26***	−.02	−.004	+.08

Note: The epistemological belief scales yield higher scores for those with more naive beliefs and lower scores for those with more mature beliefs. Therefore the correlation coefficient of −.39 between simple knowledge and intrinsic goal orientation indicates that students with more mature or sophisticated beliefs—that is, students whose lower scores indicate a belief that knowledge is complex rather than simple—are more likely to have higher scores on their intrinsic motivation scale.

* = significant at the level of .10

** = significant at the level of .05

*** = significant at the level of .01

ally, were less likely to have an intrinsic goal orientation, to appreciate the value of learning tasks, and to perceive an internal control over learning. Students with a naive belief in quick learning were also more likely than other students to have an extrinsic goal orientation toward learning. Students with the naive belief that the ability to learn is fixed were less likely to have an intrinsic goal orientation, to appreciate the value of learning tasks, to perceive an internal control over learning, and to feel efficacious about their capacity to learn than were students with the more sophisticated belief that the ability to learn can be improved (and therefore controlled) over time. Whether students believed that knowledge is absolute and certain or tentative and evolving was not found to be related to the motivational constructs, even at alpha = .1.

Discussion and Implications for Effective Teaching and Learning

Our results clearly support the findings of Hofer (1994) and of Schutz, Pintrich, and Young (1993) regarding the significant relationship between the epistemological beliefs of students and their motivation to learn in a particular course of study. Furthermore, our results expand on those of previous research, because significant relationships were observed between three of the four largely independent dimensions of epistemological beliefs (simple knowledge, quick learning, and fixed ability) and from four to six of the six distinct motivational constructs examined (intrinsic goal orientation, extrinsic goal orientation, task value, control of learning, self-efficacy, and test anxiety).

The finding that beliefs in certain knowledge are not related to students' motivation is somewhat surprising. Domain differences in the epistemological beliefs of college students provide one possible explanation, however. In a recent study, Paulsen and Wells (1998) found that among the four dimensions of epistemological beliefs, students' belief in certain knowledge showed the greatest variation across academic domains or major fields of study. Because the belief in certain knowledge is the most domain sensitive of the four dimensions, it may be that the nature of the relationship between students' beliefs in certain knowledge and their motivation is also domain specific and differs across major fields of study. If this is the case, one would then expect students' belief in certain knowledge to be related to their motivation to learn in some fields of study but not in others. Additional research is needed to further investigate this possibility.

Research on the origins and development of epistemological beliefs indicates that in addition to college experiences and educational level (Jehng, Johnson, and Anderson, 1993; Schommer, 1993), students' beliefs are shaped and formed by a variety of precollege experiences. In particular, these beliefs are related to personal and background factors, such as gender and parental education, as well as to contextual and environmental influences, such as characteristics of the early home environment, upbringing (Schommer, 1993), and precollege schooling experiences (Schommer, Calvert, Gariglietti, and Bajaj, 1997). To the extent that students' epistemological beliefs are shaped by experiences prior to college, correlations between such beliefs and students' subsequent motivation to learn in particular courses in college may be evidence of an underlying causal relationship. In other words, a causal sequence would be expected because of the presumed temporal differences in the precollege formation of epistemological beliefs and the subsequent motivation of a student to learn in a specific course in college. Although such an interpretation is necessarily speculative, it does suggest that epistemological beliefs, and their level of maturity or sophistication, may actually affect or influence students' motivation to learn.

Promoting Motivationally Productive Epistemological Beliefs

Our results suggest that college teachers can enhance the motivation of their students to learn by promoting "motivationally productive" epistemological beliefs. This would mean helping students advance from the naive beliefs that knowledge is simple, absolute, and certain, that learning takes place quickly, and that the ability to learn is fixed toward more sophisticated beliefs that knowledge is complex, tentative, and evolving, that learning takes place gradually over time, and that one's ability to learn can be improved.

Based on her analysis of the data drawn from interviews with college teachers from a variety of disciplines, Beers (1988) concluded that students' epistemological beliefs can be profoundly influenced by the instructional contexts or learning environments that faculty design for their classrooms. Beers recommends that college teachers maximize their potential to influence their students' epistemological beliefs by explicitly addressing such beliefs with students in class; that is, when an instructor "discusses the selection of course content, instructional activities, and grading with students, those discussions can be meaningfully enhanced by indicating their basis in a particular epistemological point of view" (p. 92).

On the basis of her own research and a review of the literature, Schommer (1994b) also makes recommendations for college teachers who wish to assist their students in developing more mature or sophisticated epistemological beliefs. To help students advance from the naive belief that knowledge is simple, absolute, and certain, faculty should "teach in a way that conveys learning as seeing the connections among ideas and that these connections are always evolving in nature" (p. 312). Learning activities that would be especially effective would provide opportunities for students to discover that knowledge must be adapted, or even adjusted, when applied and interpreted in different situations or contexts, thereby revealing the complex and dynamic aspects of the structure and nature of knowledge. To help students advance from the naive beliefs that learning takes place quickly or not at all and that the ability to learn is fixed, faculty should "communicate that higher level learning typically requires a struggle, and that this struggle generates emotion. . . . The response should be to work harder, longer, and to try different strategies to reach the goal" (p. 311). This can be effectively accomplished by assigning complex or even ill-structured problems that do not have straightforward solutions. Students should be encouraged to work slowly and try to find several possible solutions. With the teacher's assistance, students can then compare and contrast the various solutions to the assigned problems.

Conclusion

Faculty, in their roles as college teachers and designers of learning environments, should assume a greater responsibility for promoting motivationally and educationally productive epistemological beliefs among their students. Faculty developers can assist college teachers in doing so by giving special attention to the nature and diversity of students' epistemological beliefs in all aspects of their work with faculty—which is to say, by incorporating relevant concepts, theories, and assessments of epistemological beliefs (as connected to students' motivation and learning) into the developers' written materials, teaching seminars, orientations for new faculty and teaching assistants, one-to-one consultation with faculty, group interviews with students, and other pertinent aspects of their work as teaching consultants in campus teaching centers.

References

Bandura, A. "Self-Efficacy: Toward a Unifying Theory of Behavioral Change." *Psychological Review*, 1977, *84*, 191–215.
Beers, S. E. "Epistemological Assumptions and College Teaching: Interactions in the College Classroom." *Journal of Research in Developmental Education*, 1988, *21* (4), 87–94.

Belenky, M. F., Clinchy, B. M., Goldberger, N. R., and Tarule, J. M. *Women's Ways of Knowing*. New York: Basic Books, 1986.

Benjamin, M., McKeachie, W. J., and Lin, Y. "Two Types of Test-Anxious Students: Support for an Information Processing Model." *Journal of Educational Psychology*, 1987, *79* (2), 131–136.

Bruning, R. H., Schraw, G. J., and Ronning, R. R. *Cognitive Psychology and Instruction*. Englewood Cliffs, N.J.: Prentice Hall, 1995.

Dweck, C. S., and Elliott, E. S. "Achievement Motivation." In E. Hetherington (ed.), *Handbook of Child Psychology*. (4th ed.) New York: Wiley, 1983.

Dweck, C. S., and Leggett, E. L. "A Social-Cognitive Approach to Motivation and Personality." *Psychological Review,* 1988, *95,* 256–273.

Eccles, J. "Expectancies, Values, and Academic Behaviors." In J. Spence (ed.), *Achievement and Achievement Motives*. New York: Freeman, 1983.

Findley, M. J., and Cooper, H. M. "Locus of Control and Academic Achievement: A Literature Review." *Journal of Personality and Social Psychology*, 1983, *44* (2), 419–427.

Hofer, B. "Epistemological Beliefs and First-Year College Students: Motivation and Cognition in Different Instructional Contexts." Paper presented at the annual meeting of the American Psychological Association, Los Angeles, Aug. 1994.

Hofer, B., and Pintrich, P. R. "The Development of Epistemological Theories: Beliefs About Knowledge and Knowing and Their Relation to Learning." *Review of Educational Research,* 1997, *67* (1), 88–140.

Jehng, J. J., Johnson, S. D., and Anderson, R. C. "Schooling and Students' Epistemological Beliefs About Learning." *Contemporary Educational Psychology*, 1993, *18* (3), 23–35.

Keller, J. M. "Motivational Design of Instruction." In C. Reigeluth (ed.), *Instructional-Design Theories and Models: An Overview of Their Current Status*. Hillsdale, N.J.: Erlbaum, 1983.

Lefcourt, H. M. *Locus of Control: Current Trends in Theory and Research*. (2nd ed.) Hillsdale, N.J.: Erlbaum, 1982.

McKeachie, W. J., Pintrich, P. R., Lin, Y., Smith, D.A.F., and Sharma, R. *Teaching and Learning in the College Classroom: A Review of the Research Literature*. Ann Arbor, Mich.: National Center for Research to Improve Postsecondary Teaching and Learning, 1990.

Paulsen, M. B., and Gentry, J. A. "Motivation, Learning Strategies, and Academic Performance: A Study of the College Finance Classroom." *Financial Practice and Education,* 1995, *5* (1), 78–89.

Paulsen, M. B., and Wells, C. T. "Domain Differences in the Epistemological Beliefs of College Students." *Research in Higher Education*, 1998, *39* (4), 365–384.

Perry, W. G., Jr. *Forms of Intellectual and Ethical Development in the College Years: A Scheme*. Austin, Tex.: Holt, Rinehart and Winston, 1970.

Pintrich, P. R. "The Dynamic Interplay of Student Motivation and Cognition in the College Classroom." In M. Maehr and C. Ames (eds.), *Advances in Motivation and Achievement: Motivation Enhancing Environments*. Vol. 6. Greenwich, Conn.: JAI Press, 1989.

Pintrich, P. R., and Garcia, T. "Student Goal Orientation and Self-Regulation in the College Classroom." In M. Maehr and P. R. Pintrich (eds.), *Advances in Motivation and Achievement*. Vol. 7. Greenwich, Conn.: JAI Press, 1991.

Pintrich, P. R., and Schrauben, B. "Students' Motivational Beliefs and Their Cognitive Engagement in Classroom Academic Tasks." In D. Schunk and J. Meece (eds.), *Student Perceptions in the Classroom*. Hillsdale, N.J.: Erlbaum, 1992.

Pintrich, P. R., and Schunk, D. H. *Motivation in Education: Theory, Research, and Applications*. Englewood Cliffs, N.J.: Prentice Hall, 1996.

Pintrich, P. R., Smith, D.A.F., Garcia, T., and McKeachie, W. J. *A Manual for the Use of the Motivated Strategies for Learning Questionnaire (MSLQ)*. Ann Arbor, Mich.: National Center for Research to Improve Postsecondary Teaching and Learning, 1991.

Pintrich, P. R., Smith, D.A.F., Garcia, T., and McKeachie, W. J. "Reliability and Predictive Validity of the Motivated Strategies for Learning Questionnaire (MSLQ)." *Educational and Psychological Measurement,* 1993, *53,* 801–803.

Ryan, M. P. "Monitoring Text Comprehension: Individual Differences in Epistemological Standards." *Journal of Educational Psychology,* 1984, *76* (2), 248–258.

Schiefele, U. "Interest, Learning, and Motivation." *Educational Psychologist,* 1991, *26* (3–4), 299–323.

Schommer, M. "Effects of Beliefs About the Nature of Knowledge on Comprehension." *Journal of Educational Psychology,* 1990, *82* (3), 498–504.

Schommer, M. "Comparisons of Beliefs About the Nature of Knowledge and Learning Among Postsecondary Students." *Research in Higher Education,* 1993, *34* (3), 355–370.

Schommer, M. "An Emerging Conceptualization of Epistemological Beliefs and Their Role in Learning." In R. Garner and P. Alexander (eds.), *Beliefs About Text and About Text Instruction.* Hillsdale, N.J.: Erlbaum, 1994a.

Schommer, M. "Synthesizing Epistemological Belief Research: Tentative Understandings and Provocative Confusions." *Educational Psychology Review,* 1994b, *6* (4), 293–319.

Schommer, M., Calvert, C., Gariglietti, G., and Bajaj, A. "The Development of Epistemological Beliefs Among Secondary Students: A Longitudinal Study." *Journal of Educational Psychology,* 1997, *89* (1), 37–40.

Schutz, P. A., Pintrich, P. R., and Young, A. J. "Epistemological Beliefs, Motivation, and Student Learning." Paper presented at the annual meeting of the American Educational Research Association, Atlanta, Apr. 1993.

MICHAEL B. PAULSEN *is professor of educational leadership at the University of New Orleans.*

KENNETH A. FELDMAN *is professor of sociology at the State University of New York at Stony Brook.*

Motivation for higher-order learning and for lifelong learning are essential outcomes in postsecondary education. Students' motivation and strategies for studying and their learning goals interact with the learning context. These relationships suggest new perspectives for research on student learning.

Motivation for Higher-Order Learning

Janet G. Donald

For faculty, the ideal student is one who actively seeks intellectual challenge. According to university graduates, undergraduates, and stakeholders in postsecondary education, higher-order learning and a commitment to learning are the most important criteria of quality for postsecondary students (Donald and Denison, 1996, 1997; Evers and Gilbert, 1991). Higher-order learning includes problem solving, critical thinking, synthesis and evaluation, and oral and written expression. The aim of this chapter is to increase our understanding of student motivation and its relationship to higher-order learning. A further aim is to extend the dialogue on the effect of context on motivation, to test the hypothesis that context affects motivation and hence learning outcomes.

The concept of student motivation is polymorphous, containing attitudes, goals, and strategies. At the broadest level of analysis, in studies on intellectual development (Perry, 1970, 1981) and student quality (Donald and Denison, 1997), student motivation has been conceptualized as a commitment to learning. At a second, more specific level, originating in phenomenological research on how students experience the learning process (Marton and Saljo, 1976), is literature on students' approaches or orientations to learning and studying. In the orientation literature, student motivation and strategies are most frequently measured in inventories. At a third level of specificity is work on intrinsic and extrinsic motivation for learning, which Paulsen and Feldman have related to students' epistemological beliefs in Chapter Two of this volume. At the most specific level is work on learning goals, particularly higher-order learning goals in courses in different disciplines. For example, Cashin and Downey's (1995)

This chapter is based on research funded by the Quebec Fonds pour la Formation de Chercheurs et l'Aide à la Recherche and the Social Sciences and Humanities Research Council of Canada.

study of students' perceptions of what they learn reveals emphasis on different higher-order goals across domains. The research reported in this chapter takes into account factors that have been shown to affect higher-order learning: students' program and preparation for studies, their motivation for studying, their strategies and learning goals, and the learning context.

The Relationship of Motivation to Higher-Order Learning

Learning goals in postsecondary education include gaining factual knowledge but also more demanding higher-order goals such as learning principles, problem solving, synthesis and evaluation, and written, oral, and independent work skills. Students need to be aware of these higher-order learning goals in order to take responsibility for their learning, that is, to assume self-control, to self-regulate. In our studies of criteria of student quality, students assigned the greatest importance to a commitment to learning and the ability to analyze, synthesize, and think critically (Donald and Denison, 1997). In principal components analysis, these criteria were associated in the same component.

International research on student approaches or orientations to learning utilizes the term *orientation* to indicate a combination of an approach to studying, style of learning, and motivation that is relatively stable across different educational tasks (Biggs, 1988, 1993; Entwistle and Tait, 1990; Meyer, Parsons, and Dunne, 1990; Ramsden, 1992). In early work (Entwistle and Ramsden, 1983), four student orientations were proposed: meaning (deep), reproducing (surface), achieving (competitive and grade oriented), and nonacademic (negative attitudes and disorganized study methods). These orientations were held to influence student success in learning. Generally speaking, this research suggests that students' deep motivation and strategies for learning are associated with higher-order learning. Research more specifically focused on the effect of motivation on learning has examined intrinsic and extrinsic motivation and strategies for improving learning (Astin, 1993; Pintrich, 1995; Pintrich, Brown, and Weinstein, 1994; Pintrich, Marx, and Boyle, 1993; Stage and Williams, 1990). Intrinsic motivation for learning is defined as the desire to learn for the sake of understanding; extrinsic motivation is defined as a desire to attain an external goal. Astin (1993) found that some students, labeled *scholars*, adopted a deep or meaning approach to learning, expected to succeed, spent more time studying, and most significantly in terms of this study, reported improvement in their problem-solving skills and critical thinking ability. In contrast, *uncommitted* students failed to complete assignments on time, were bored in class, and were more likely to report feeling overwhelmed by all they had to do.

The Effect of Context on Motivation for Higher-Order Learning

Programs and the individual courses within them create two sets of context effects that interact with student motivation and strategies and thus affect learning outcomes. First, disciplines provide learning climates that are distinctive in their learning goals and instructional methods (Cashin and Downey, 1995). For example, physical scientists emphasize facts, principles, and problem solving while in the social sciences and humanities a critical perspective and communication skills are important (Stark, Shaw, and Lowther, 1989). Second, students have particular characteristics that interact with the learning context. In one study (Garcia and Pintrich, 1992), natural science students exhibited both higher motivation and more learning strategies than social science students, but the level of motivation was a significant predictor of higher-order learning for both natural and social science students.

Research also suggests that some students are flexible and may adopt approaches according to their goals and what they perceive the instructor's expectations or evaluation plans to be (Entwistle and Tait, 1990; Ramsden, 1992). In one study, in which student motivation for deep and achieving motives decreased over the semester, the researchers argued that because two different groups of students in the course displayed the same pattern of decreasing motivation, the course context rather than individual student characteristics led to changes in student motivation (Volet, Renshaw, and Tietzel, 1994). The research on student motivation and learning goals thus suggests a set of factors that affect student higher-order learning: students' characteristics (including their preparation and program of studies), their motivation and strategies for learning, the learning goals in the course, and the extent to which students are aware of the learning goals. In this study, a short-term longitudinal design was used to examine the relative effects of course and program on student motivation over a semester in an introductory physics course. Physics was chosen as the subject matter area because of the emphasis placed on higher-order learning in the discipline (Donald, 1993).

Procedure

Students gave their perceptions of learning in questionnaires administered in the third week of the semester and again at the end of the course. At the beginning of the term, deep, surface, and achieving motives and strategies were explored using the Study Process Questionnaire (Biggs, 1988) and intrinsic and extrinsic motivation were measured using items from the Motivated Strategies for Learning Questionnaire (MSLQ) (Pintrich, 1987). Students were also asked to indicate the emphasis they placed on different learning goals in the course. The end-of-term questionnaire included the items on intrinsic and extrinsic motivation and items on students' progress in achieving the learning goals. Measures of students' entering average grade, their expected grade, and their final grade in the course were also obtained.

A sample of thirty-nine students filled in both the beginning and end-of-term questionnaires, 56 percent of seventy students enrolled in the course. The sample was representative of the class based on final course grade (73 percent for sample and class) and student demographics. Just over half the students

(21 or 54 percent) indicated a program in the physical sciences; the remaining eighteen indicated an engineering program. We thus had samples of students from two comparable programs, that is, both "hard" but one pure and one applied according to the Biglan (1973) scheme, in a course recommended for both programs but taught in the physics department.

Student Preparation

In spite of high entering averages (91 percent mean for engineering students and 87 percent mean for physical science students), students were cautious in their estimation of preparation for their chosen field, with 56 percent of students considering themselves well prepared. More physics students (76 percent) felt more well prepared for the course than for their program, while engineering students felt equally well prepared for the course and for their program. Although engineering students had an advantage in their entering average, more physics students felt prepared for the course than did engineering students. Students' perceptions of their preparation for the course thus appeared to be based more on their degree of identification with the discipline than on their own previous performance.

Students' Learning Motives

In their approaches to studying, students considered two achieving motive items to be most true of themselves: "I have a strong desire to excel in all of my studies" and "I want top grades in most or all of my courses so that I will be able to select from among the best positions available when I graduate." The next most frequently chosen items were a surface strategy ("I learn best from teachers who work from carefully prepared notes and outline major points neatly on the blackboard"), a deep strategy ("I try to relate new material, as I am reading it, to what I already know on that topic"), and a deep motive ("I usually become increasingly absorbed in my work the more I do"). Physical science students displayed the classic scholar's approach, endorsing deep motives and strategies and achieving motives and strategies more than surface motives and strategies. Engineering students were more eclectic in their motives and in their willingness to employ a variety of strategies. Their achieving motive was higher than their deep motive, but they otherwise did not show differences between deep, achieving, and surface motives or strategies. Both physical science and engineering students displayed greater intrinsic than extrinsic motivation on the MSLQ items. Students' scores for intrinsic motivation correlated significantly with deep motivation and strategies and with achieving strategies. This was consistent with the research on a generalized deep approach to learning (Biggs, 1988). Negative correlations were found, as expected, between intrinsic motivation and surface motivation and strategies. Thus the intrinsic motivation scores were measuring the same construct as the generalized deep approach. In contrast, extrinsic motivation correlated with achieving and surface motivation, confirming the generalized surface approach to studying found in results using the Study Process Questionnaire (Biggs and Rihn, 1984; O'Neil and Child, 1984).

Changes over the Term in Learning Motives

Physical science and engineering students' intrinsic learning motives decreased significantly over the term. The greatest change was in the importance of understanding the subject matter of the course—an issue crucial to higher-order learning. Students also showed decreases in extrinsic motivation, especially in competitive spirit. More striking was the relative change in intrinsic and extrinsic motivation. At the beginning of the term, both physical science and engineering students displayed greater intrinsic than extrinsic motivation. This remained true for physical science students, but by the end of the term engineering students displayed equal intrinsic and extrinsic motivation and their main goal was to get a good grade rather than to understand the subject matter of the course. Our results suggest an attribute-treatment interaction in which higher achieving motivation on the part of engineering students at the beginning of the term develops into a primary focus on getting a good grade at the end of the term. The results are also consistent with the decrease in deep and achieving motives for students over a semester that Volet, Renshaw, and Tietzel (1994) attribute to students' perceptions of course requirements and that Cote and Levine (1997) explain as lowering their sights.

Students' Learning Goals and Outcomes

If students need to be aware of higher-order learning goals in order to take responsibility for their learning, the emphasis they place on different learning goals is an important factor in their development. At the beginning of the term, students placed moderate or very heavy emphasis on higher-order goals, most frequently emphasizing learning fundamental principles, concepts, or theories, followed by learning how to problem solve and how to synthesize or evaluate (see Table 3.1). Thus students were attuned to the higher-order learning challenge. Fewer students emphasized learning how to study independently and learning factual knowledge, and only a small percentage emphasized learning how to organize and present ideas in written form and orally. There were no differences across programs in the emphasis students placed on these learning goals, but students clearly differentiated between the goals at both the beginning and the end of the term. Moreover, the relative emphasis placed on goals remained remarkably consistent. The only exceptions over the term were physical science students' reduced emphasis on learning principles and oral skills; engineering students showed no significant changes. Students felt, however, that their progress did not match their emphasis on the learning goals; compared to the emphasis they placed on these goals at the beginning of the

Table 3.1. Students' Emphasis on Different Learning Goals over a Term

Learning Goal	Time	Physical Science		Engineering	
		Mean	SD	Mean	SD
1. Learning fundamental principles, concepts, or theories	Beginning of Term	4.86	.36	4.67	.49
	End of Term	4.48**	.60	4.61	.61
BoT & EoT: 1 > 3, 4, 5, 6, 7***; BoT: 1 > 2					
2. Learning how to problem solve	Beginning of Term	4.57	.68	4.56	.51
	End of Term	4.62	.67	4.67	.77
BoT: 2 > 4, 5, 6, 7***, 2 > 3**					
EoT: 2 > 3, 4, 5, 6, 7***					
3. Learning how to synthesize or evaluate	Beginning of Term	4.10	.83	4.22	.81
	End of Term	3.95	.97	4.00	.91
BoT: 3 > 5, 6, 7***;					
EoT: 3 > 6, 7***, 3 > 4, 5*					
4. Learning how to study or work independently	Beginning of Term	3.86	1.39	3.67	1.08
	End of Term	3.52	1.12	3.44	1.29
BoT: 4 > 6, 7***;					
EoT: 4 > 6**, 4 > 7***					
5. Learning factual knowledge (terminology, classification)	Beginning of Term	3.71	.72	3.44	.92
	End of Term	3.67	1.06	3.44	1.15
BoT & EoT: 5 > 6**, 5 > 7***					
6. Learning how to organize and present ideas in written form	Beginning of Term	3.05	.97	3.00	.91
	End of Term	2.95	1.12	2.56	1.29
BoT & EoT: 6 > 7***					
7. Learning how to organize and present ideas orally	Beginning of Term	2.57	1.12	2.22	1.06
	End of Term	1.90*	1.04	1.94	1.26

Note: Scores were based on the following scale: 1 = none; 2 = a little; 3 = some; 4 = moderate; 5 = very heavy emphasis.

$*\ p < .05$

$**\ p < .01$

$***\ p < .001$

term, they reported significantly lower progress for learning principles, problem solving, and synthesis. Intrinsic and extrinsic motivation did not correlate significantly with final grade, but students' sense of having been prepared for the course and their program did. The best predictor of final grade for physical science students was their felt preparation for the course at the beginning of the term, while for engineering students the best predictor was their entering average. This contrast in predictors reflects the difference in familiarity of disciplinary context: physical science students achieved according to their fit with the course context, while engineering students achieved in accordance with their previous performance.

Implications

A major intent of this study was to increase understanding of student motivation and its relationship to higher-order learning. At a general level, the measures of student motivation, both students' intrinsic or deep motivation and strategies for learning, are associated with higher-order learning, most strongly reflected in students' desire to understand the subject matter of the course. At a more specific level, intrinsic motivation correlates with higher-order learning goals, but the relationship is not as strong. Context and student preparation have a greater effect on achievement than does motivation. More telling, students within the discipline felt that preparation for the course was the best predictor of success as measured by final grade. For students from the parallel applied discipline, their previous level of achievement best predicted their course outcome. These results tell us that students' perceptions of their preparation may be more concise indicators of their achievement in courses than measures of their motivation or learning goals. As instructors, we therefore may learn from students' entering characteristics, and paying attention to these characteristics, as Wlodkowski suggests in Chapter One of this volume, may improve learning outcomes.

The results also tell us that we need to know more specifically what course goals are important to the instructor, if these change throughout the term, and if students recognize them as fitting the activities and evaluation procedures in the course. Students placed significantly different degrees of emphasis on different learning goals in the course, and they maintained these differences over the term. They placed very heavy emphasis on both conceptual learning and learning how to problem solve throughout the course. Their progress, however, was significantly lower, according to their reports. The changes in student motivation and the limited progress over the semester should ring warning bells. Fewer students were intrinsically motivated at the end of the course than at the beginning of the term, and although they continued to emphasize higher-order learning goals, they reported progress with them less frequently. The interaction between program and changes in intrinsic motivation, in which engineering students but not physical science students changed from being more intrinsically motivated to being more extrinsically motivated, suggests a different kind of commitment to learning in the course. The engineering students' entering average grade (higher) and felt preparation for the course (lower) conflict as indicators of course achievement in comparison with those for the physical science students, and the higher correlation of entering average with final grade for engineering students coupled with increased extrinsic motivation suggests an overall greater distance from the discipline and an accompanying instrumentalism on their part. Thus, for physical science students the context appeared to have a greater effect, and although intrinsic motivation decreased over the semester, it sill remained the dominant motivation. Students from a different program, however, were more context independent, and although their emphasis on learning goals paralleled that of the physical science students, their motivation changed. The results also point to the need to explore the causes of the decrease in intrinsic motivation.

Students have reported adjustments in their expectations (Donald, 1994, 1997), but we need to know to what extent these stem from unrealistic expectations of a course or if greater attention to students' intrinsic motivation and higher-order goals on the part of instructors would affect the way students respond to the demands of a course. More generally, we need to understand how courses and programs are sequenced and how this affects student learning. Our ongoing research on the learning climate and higher-order learning in specific disciplines seeks to answer these questions.

References

Astin, A. "An Empirical Typology of College Students." *Journal of College Student Development*, 1993, *34*, 36–46.

Biggs, J. B. *The Study Process Questionnaire (SPQ): User's Manual*. Hawthorn, Victoria: Australian Council for Educational Research, 1988.

Biggs, J. B. "What Do Inventories of Students' Learning Processes Really Measure? A Theoretical Review and Clarification." *British Journal of Educational Psychology*, 1993, *63*, 3–19.

Biggs, J. B., and Rihn, B. A. "The Effects of Interventions on Deep and Surface Approaches to Learning." In J. R. Kirby (ed.), *Cognitive Strategies and Educational Performance*. Orlando, Fla.: Academic Press, 1984.

Biglan, A. "The Characteristics of Subject Matter in Different Academic Areas." *Journal of Applied Psychology*, 1973, *57* (3), 195–203.

Cashin, W. E., and Downey, R. G. "Disciplinary Differences in What Is Taught and in Students' Perceptions of What They Learn and How They Are Taught." In N. Hativa and M. Marincovich (eds.), *Disciplinary Differences in Teaching and Learning*. New Directions for Teaching and Learning, no. 64. San Francisco: Jossey-Bass, 1995.

Cote, J. E., and Levine, C. "Student Motivations, Learning Environments, and Human Capital Acquisition: Toward an Integrated Paradigm of Student Development." *Journal of College Student Development*, 1997, *38*, 229–243.

Donald, J. G. "Professors' and Students' Conceptualizations of the Learning Task in Physics Courses." *Journal of Research on Science Teaching*, 1993, *30*, 905–918.

Donald, J. G. "Science Students' Learning: Ethnographic Studies in Three Disciplines." In P. Pintrich, D. Brown, and C. Weinstein (eds.), *Student Motivation, Cognition, and Learning*. Hillsdale, N.J.: Erlbaum, 1994.

Donald, J. G. *Improving the Environment for Learning: Academic Leaders Talk About What Works*. San Francisco: Jossey-Bass, 1997.

Donald, J. G., and Denison, D. B. "Evaluating Undergraduate Education: The Use of Broad Indicators." *Assessment and Evaluation in Higher Education*, 1996, *21* (1), 23–39.

Donald, J. G., and Denison, D. B. "Assessing the Quality of University Students: Student Perceptions of Quality Criteria." Paper presented at the annual meeting of the American Educational Research Association, Chicago, Mar. 1997.

Entwistle, N. J., and Ramsden, P. *Understanding Student Learning*. London: Croom Helm, 1983.

Entwistle, N. J., and Tait, H. "Approaches to Learning, Evaluations of Teaching, and Preferences for Contrasting Academic Environments." *Higher Education*, 1990, *19*, 169–194.

Evers, F. T., and Gilbert, S. "Outcomes Assessment: How Much Value Does University Education Add?" *Canadian Journal of Higher Education*, 1991, *12* (2), 53–76.

Garcia, T., and Pintrich, P. *Critical Thinking and Its Relationship to Motivation, Learning Strategies, and Classroom Experience*. Symposium on Learning, Thinking, and Problem-Solving

Issues in Teaching and Transfer, conducted at the annual meeting of the American Psychological Association, Washington, D.C., Aug. 1992.

Marton, F., and Saljo, R. "On Qualitative Differences in Learning. I. Outcome and Process." *British Journal of Educational Psychology,* 1976, *46,* 4–11.

Meyer, J.H.F., Parsons, P., and Dunne, T. T. "Individual Study Orchestrations and Their Association with Learning Outcome." *Higher Education,* 1990, *20,* 67–89.

O'Neil, M. J., and Child, D. "Biggs' SPQ: A British Study of Its Internal Structure." *British Journal of Educational Psychology,* 1984, *54,* 228–234.

Perry, W. G. *Forms of Intellectual and Ethical Development in the College Years: A Scheme.* Austin, Tex.: Holt, Rinehart and Winston, 1970.

Perry, W. G. "Intellectual and Ethical Development." In A. W. Chickering and Associates, *The Modern American College: Responding to the New Realities of Diverse Students and a Changing Society.* San Francisco: Jossey-Bass, 1981.

Pintrich, P. R. "Motivated Learning Strategies in the College Classroom." Paper presented at the annual meeting of the American Educational Research Association, Washington, D.C., 1987.

Pintrich, P. R. (ed.). *Understanding Self-Regulated Learning.* New Directions for Teaching and Learning, no. 63. San Francisco: Jossey-Bass, 1995.

Pintrich, P. R., Brown, D., and Weinstein, C. (eds.). *Student Motivation, Cognition, and Learning.* Hillsdale, N.J.: Erlbaum, 1994.

Pintrich, P. R., Marx, R. W., and Boyle, R. A. "Beyond Cold Conceptual Change: The Role of Motivational Beliefs and Classroom Contextual Factors in the Process of Conceptual Change." *Review of Educational Research,* 1993, *63* (2), 167–199.

Ramsden, P. *Learning to Teach in Higher Education.* New York: Routledge, 1992.

Ramsden, P., and Entwistle, N. J. "Effects of Academic Departments on Students' Approaches to Studying." *British Journal of Educational Psychology,* 1981, *51,* 368–383.

Stage, F. K., and Williams, P. D. "Students' Motivations and Changes in Motivation During the First Year of College." *Journal of College Student Development,* 1990, *31,* 516–522.

Stark, J. S., Shaw, K. M., and Lowther, M. A. *Student Goals for College and Courses.* Report no. 6. Washington D.C.: School of Education and Human Development, George Washington University, 1989.

Volet, S. E., Renshaw, P. D., and Tietzel, K. "A Short-Term Longitudinal Investigation of Cross-Cultural Differences in Study Approaches Using Biggs' SPQ Questionnaire." *British Journal of Educational Psychology,* 1994, *64,* 301–318.

JANET G. DONALD *is director of the Graduate Program in Cognition and Instruction at McGill University in Montreal and is former director of the Centre for University Teaching and Learning.*

PART TWO

Motivation and Methods

This chapter describes the application of an instructional design process that provides methods and guidelines for incorporating motivational tactics into computer-based and distance learning environments.

Using the ARCS Motivational Process in Computer-Based Instruction and Distance Education

John M. Keller

It is one thing to design for learner motivation in a classroom setting where teachers or facilitators can respond to changes as soon as they sense them. It is a greater challenge to make self-directed learning environments responsive to the motivational requirements of learners. It requires both a systematic motivational design process that provides adequate guidelines and methods of incorporating feasible and effective motivational tactics into the environment, and knowledge of the dynamics of human motivation.

The ARCS model of motivational design (Keller, 1987a, 1987b) provides a systematic, seven-step approach (Keller, 1997) to designing motivational tactics into instruction. It incorporates needs assessment based on an analysis of the target audience and existing instructional materials, supports the creation of motivational objectives and measures based on an analysis of the motivational characteristics of the learners, provides guidance for creating and selecting motivational tactics, and follows a process that integrates well with instructional design and development. The analysis of motivational needs and corresponding selection of tactics are based on four dimensions of motivation. These dimensions were derived from a synthesis of research on human motivation and are known as attention (A), relevance (R), confidence (C), and satisfaction (S), or ARCS. Numerous reports and studies have described and confirmed the validity of this model (for example, Means, Jonassen, and Dwyer, 1997; Small and Gluck, 1994; and Visser and Keller, 1990).

This model has been applied to various types of learning environments, such as classroom instruction, self-paced print, computer-based instruction

(CBI), and multimedia, but these applications have been limited in scope and function. Furthermore, the full seven-step model can be time-consuming and confusing to a person who is not trained in its use. A recent development in Japan (Suzuki and Keller, 1996; Keller, 1997) provides a simplified and effective approach to motivational design and has subsequently been applied in two innovative applications to the improvement of self-directed learning. The first application was to the development of motivationally adaptive CBI (Song, 1998). In addition to incorporating the simplified motivational design approach, this application builds on concepts and approaches initiated in the United Kingdom and Italy by del Soldato and du Boulay (1995) and in Austria by Astleitner and Keller (1995). The prototype of the adaptive CBI was developed in the United States and will be cross-validated in Korea. The second application was in the student support methods for a distance learning course in Europe (Visser, 1998). It is interesting to note the multinational representation in these studies.

In Sendai, Japan, a team of twenty-five teachers in eight subject areas at Sendai Daichi Junior High School had been developing computer application projects for several years as part of a demonstration project sponsored by the Japanese national government. During the last two years of the project, they were asked to incorporate systematic motivational design into their process. Suzuki (Suzuki and Keller, 1996) developed a simplified approach to motivational design because the full seven-step model would require too much time for training and implementation. The goal of the simplified approach was to ensure that the teachers would identify key motivational characteristics in the learners, in the content area to be taught, and in the hardware or software to be used. The teachers then evaluated this information and prescribed tactics based on identified motivational problems. This process helped to ensure that teachers avoided the inclusion of excessive numbers of tactics or of tactics derived from their own preferred areas of interest without regard to the characteristics of the students and the situation.

The resulting design process is represented in a matrix (Table 4.1). In the first row, the designer lists salient characteristics of the learners' overall motivation to learn. The second row contains the designer's judgments about how appealing the learning task will be to the learners. The third and fourth rows ask about learners' expected attitudes toward the medium of instruction and the instructional materials. Each of the entries in these rows has a plus or minus sign to indicate whether it is a positive or negative motivational characteristic. Based on the information provided in these first three rows, the motivational designers decide how much motivational support is required and what types of tactics to use. They refer to reference lists of potential tactics (for example, Keller and Burkman, 1993; Keller and Suzuki, 1988) and also create their own tactics based on the identified needs.

In this example, the teacher determined that confidence is the only real problem area and he listed some specific things to deal with it. He also listed some specific tactics for the other categories, but they serve to maintain motivation instead of solving a specific problem.

Table 4.1.   ARCS Motivational Design Matrix 1: Elective Unit on Using International E-mail

Design Factors	ARCS Categories			
	Attention	Relevance	Confidence	Satisfaction
Learner characteristics	Elective course, high interest (+)	High commitment (+)	Low skills in typing and in conversational English (−)	Newly formed group of students (−) but familiar teacher (+)
Learning task (Learners' attitudes toward)	New, attractive, adventurous (+)	High public interest to the Internet (+) Useful in future (+) Limited access to computers (−)	Seems difficult (−) First exposure (−)	High applicability of acquired skills (+) Exciting outcome (+)
Medium: Computer in this lesson (Learners' attitudes toward)	Interesting new use as a networking tool (+)	Familiar as a stand-alone learning tool (+)	Unstable network connection may make students worried (−)	Immediate feedback (+)
Courseware characteristics (e-mail software)			English usage (−)	Participatory for every student (+)
Motivational tactics for the lesson	Minimal tactics required: Emphasize opportunity to communicate worldwide Demonstrate immediate transmission and response features	Minimal tactics required: Demonstrate how it extends one's communication capabilities	Necessary to build confidence: Set objectives cumulatively from low to high Team teaching with an assistant English teacher Use translation software	Minimal tactics required: Provide reinforcement by receiving messages from "network pals"

A benefit of his application of this process was that in his initial motivational plan, created before he applied this process, he had a much longer list of tactics that he thought would be exciting and motivational. After doing the analysis and applying various selection criteria that are listed in the training materials on motivational design, he realized that his list of tactics would be too time-consuming and would actually distract from the students' intrinsic interest in the subject as revealed in his analysis. By using the design process, he was able to simplify the motivational design and target it to specific needs.

An evaluation of the effectiveness of this motivational design process (Suzuki and Keller, 1996) verified that the teachers were able to use the matrix accurately, with only a few entries not being placed appropriately, and more than two-thirds felt that it definitely helped them produce a more effective motivational design. Some teachers had difficulties with the analysis phase, which indicates that this is a critical area to address in training people to use the process.

This simplified design process was modified and used in two subsequent projects. The first of these was to develop a prototype of motivationally adaptive CBI. The formal motivational design process requires an audience analysis, which influences which motivational tactics will be included in the learning environment. Learner motivation changes over time, however, and sometimes in unpredictable ways. In a classroom or other instructor-led setting, an expert instructor can continuously gauge the audience's motivational condition and make adjustments as appropriate. But in self-directed learning environments, this type of continuous adjustment has not been a feature. Once the instruction has been designed and "packaged," everyone receives the same program, with the exception of limited branching and other learner-control options. These options can have a positive effect on motivation, but they do not adequately reflect the range of motivational conditions that characterize learners at different points in time.

It would be possible to include a large number of motivational tactics to cover a broad range of motivational conditions, but this would most likely have a negative effect on motivation and performance. The reason is that when students are motivated to learn, they want to work on highly task-relevant activities. They do not want to be distracted with unnecessary motivational activities. For this reason it would be nice to have computer or multimedia software that can sense a learner's motivation level and respond adaptively.

Song (1998) designed and tested an approach to motivationally adaptive computer-based instruction. He built checkpoints into an instructional program on genetics for junior high school students. At predetermined points, students in the primary treatment group received a screen asking several questions about their motivational attitudes. Based on the responses, which were compared to actual performance levels, students would receive motivational tactics designed to improve attention, relevance, or confidence. Song used a variation of the simplified ARCS model design process to create specifications for tactics to be included in the adaptive treatment. The resulting motivation and performance of this group were compared to those of a group that received highly efficient instruction with only a minimum of motivational tactics that centered primarily on acceptable screen layout. A second comparison group received the maximum number of tactics; that is, they received all of the tactics that were in the pool of potential tactics for the treatment group.

The results indicated that both the adaptive and full-featured treatments were superior to the minimalist treatment. In most instances, the adaptive treatment was superior to the full-featured one. There were limitations on the types of computer features that could be used in this study (for example, there was no sound), but based on these results, a more sophisticated treatment and also one that was longer than one hour would be expected to show even stronger treatment effects.

This study was a pioneering effort. Earlier papers that discussed or tested adaptive motivational design (Astleitner and Keller, 1995; del Soldato and du Boulay, 1995) were extremely rigorous but more limited in their approach; that is, they tended to focus on a particular aspect of motivation, such as persistence or confidence. Song's study is more holistic and provides a good foundation for a series of follow-up studies. One of the first of these will be a cross-cultural development and comparison to be conducted in Korea.

The second extension of the simplified design process is in distance learning (Visser, 1998) and provides another example of the multicultural nature of this work. Visser, who lives in France, conducted her research with a distance learning course offered by a university in the United Kingdom and is working under the sponsorship of her university in the Netherlands. Furthermore, her study includes an adaptation of a motivational strategy developed and validated in an adult education setting in Mozambique (Visser and Keller, 1990).

There is no doubt that there are serious motivational challenges among distance learners. The attrition rate alone can be viewed as an indication of motivational problems. Students' comments often focus on their feelings of isolation, lack of feeling of making steady progress, and great doubts about being able to finish the course given their other responsibilities and time constraints. Visser (1998) used the simplified ARCS model design process to analyze the audience, conditions, and potential solutions. Her application of this process was contextualized in two ways. First, it was restricted to a somewhat formal and traditional distance learning course that uses textual material supplemented by an occasional audiocassette or videocassette. Based on her global assessment of the motivational problems in this situation, she concluded that it might be possible to have a positive effect on motivation by focusing on the student support system rather than on the instruction, which could not be revised easily.

The second way in which her study is contextualized is in its focus on the validation of a particular motivational strategy, although it does allow for the incorporation of multiple tactics. Her approach was to implement a program of "motivational messages" that would be sent to students according to two schedules. The first schedule was a set of fixed points based on predictions of the points during the course when these messages might have the strongest effect. The messages were the same for everyone. The second schedule consisted of personal messages sent to students when the tutor deemed it appropriate. These messages were in the form of greeting cards, which conveyed messages of encouragement, reminders, empathy, advice, and other appropriate content areas.

Design of the messages was based on the results of her application of the simplified design process (see Table 4.2), in which she changed some of the specific design factors while keeping their basic intent. The first two rows contain predictions of students' entering attitudes toward distance learning in general and of what their attitudes might be after they have been in the course for

Table 4.2. Mini-Design for the Development of Motivational Messages in Distance Education Courses

| Design Factors | ARCS Categories | | | |
	Attention	Relevance	Confidence	Satisfaction
Precourse attitudes of students toward distance learning	New students: strong in the beginning (new materials/new topic), gradually diminishing as novelty wears off. Probably low level of attention for repeaters.	Decision to take the course is, most of the time, voluntary, not imposed. No big problems expected in relevance. May improve as learners apply what they have learned, or decrease if not what was expected.	A very sensitive area, as the mode of instruction is new and unfamiliar. Generally satisfactory for experienced and successful distance education learners. Repeaters anxious about pitfalls; newcomers uncertain. Also, there is no peer support.	Successful completion of the course is an important step in the direction of a degree.
Midterm attitudes toward distance learning	Initially high attention and curiosity wear off as courses are often not really exciting and sometimes even boring.	Continues to provide an interesting possibility to make a career move or to show what has been learned. Time conflicts with other activities occur.	If they are confident in the beginning, this wears off. Evaluation system is not very encouraging. No motivational support included in course. Very low level of confidence for beginners.	Reasonable, but dissatisfaction sometimes sets in. Both repeaters and new students soon disappointed about the limited interaction and about studying in isolation.
Student reactions to this course content	Initially high, but soon decreases due to lack of novelty and variation in content and learning strategies.	Course content is relevant, but too little interactivity to help students learn how to apply it. Some material is outdated.	Confidence that it can be done soon fades due to volume of work, lack of support, and lack of opportunity to see growth and application.	Remains reasonable.
Characteristics of student support during the course	Minimal, only contact is through feedback on assignments. Nothing unusual or unexpected happens.	Feedback is usually limited strictly to course content. No creative feedback to show connections to students.	Feedback is mostly worded in a positive way, but occasionally too general.	Low because of lack of meaningful and personal contact.

Table 4.2. (continued)

Summary	Initial attention soon slips.	Relevance usually continues through the course, although it becomes less important.	Confidence depends heavily on results, but is generally low. This area needs extensive motivational treatment.	Satisfaction is not a big problem, or would not be if the other issues were resolved.
Examples of motivational tactics to be used in motivational messages	Bring pacing into the course and offer tutor's assistance. Use student's name and include personal comments in feedback messages. Provide an unexpected communication to students from time to time.	Provide occasional extra material such as a publication. Provide creative feedback and link feedback to learner's work and daily circumstances.	Emphasize that they can do it if effort is put into the course. Reassure the learners by showing personal interest and concern. Make them feel part of a group who are all struggling to get it done. Show empathy. Provide encouragement and personal challenges at times that are known to be low points in the term.	Make turnaround time for assignments short. Ensure that tutors are accessible. Refer to positive feelings a learner will have when the course is completed successfully. Reward early completion through complimenting learners personally.

a while. Designers' responses to these questions will come primarily from the instructor's background experiences with the target audience. The third row predicts attitudes toward the course content, and the fourth row asks about students' attitudes toward the support they receive while taking the course. Visser's fifth row is new. It provides an opportunity to summarize the results of the first four rows. In the earlier version of the matrix (Table 4.1), the summarizing comments were included with the motivational tactic recommendations in the final row. As in that version, the final row in this table contains a general summary of tactics or tactic considerations to guide the detailed design process. Visser included statements of both positive and negative features of each situation and did not use the convention of pluses and minuses.

To assess the effectiveness of this intervention, Visser compared retention rates in the experimental section of the course to three other sections that did not receive motivational messages, and she did a qualitative review of students' responses to various course evaluation and feedback instruments. She did not ask students directly about the effects of the motivational messages to avoid stimulating attitudes that may not have been present spontaneously in the students' minds. Improved retention rates of 70 to 80 percent, which are similar to conventional education, and student comments both offered clear support for the motivational messages.

These three studies have extended systematic motivational design in three directions. The first is further refinement of systematic approaches to motivational design. In this case, the simplified model provides an efficient and effective means of supporting educators in improving the motivational aspects of learning environments. It is to be stressed, however, that in each case there were one or more persons who had expert knowledge of motivational theory and application. It remains to be seen how effectively the simplified design process can be used by persons with no knowledge of the research and theory behind the four dimensions of motivation (attention, relevance, confidence, and satisfaction) or knowledge of the detailed elements of the motivational design process.

The second extension of motivational design refers to contexts of application. These studies illustrate how systematic motivational design can be incorporated into formal instructional design and curriculum development projects, how it can serve as a basis for motivationally adaptive CBI, and how it can increase student motivation and performance by improving the student support system in distance learning.

The final extension is the multicultural one. The ARCS model, together with other approaches to motivational improvement, is being used in many different countries in the world, but there are few publications that describe systematic applications. The studies in this report encompass at least five different countries in Asia and Europe and illustrate that the basic process can apply multinationally.

In conclusion, motivation, which has traditionally been viewed by many people as an "untouchable," that is, as a highly idiosyncratic and variable condition, can be approached systematically. Research on motivation and motivational design shows that there are stable elements of motivation, and even some of the unstable elements are predictable. Educators can manage learning environments to stimulate and sustain motivation, even though they cannot control it. Ultimately, each human being is responsible for his or her motivational condition, but it is abundantly clear that the environment can have a strong impact on both the direction and intensity of a person's motivation.

References

Astleitner, J., and Keller, J. M. "A Model for Motivationally Adaptive Computer-Assisted Instruction." *Journal of Research on Computing in Education,* 1995, 27 (3), 270–280.

del Soldato, T., and du Boulay, B. "Implementation of Motivational Tactics in Tutoring Systems." *Journal of Artificial Intelligence in Education,* 1995, 6 (4), 337–338.

Keller, J. M. "Strategies for Stimulating the Motivation to Learn." *Performance and Instruction,* 1987a, 26 (8), 1–7.

Keller, J. M. "The Systematic Process of Motivational Design." *Performance and Instruction,* 1987b, 26 (9), 1–8.

Keller, J. M. "Motivational Design and Multimedia: Beyond the Novelty Effect." *Strategic Human Resource Development Review,* 1997, 1 (1), 188–203.

Keller, J. M., and Burkman, E. "Motivation Principles." In M. Fleming and W. H. Levie (eds.), *Instructional Message Design: Principles from the Behavioral and Cognitive Sciences.* Englewood Cliffs, N.J.: Educational Technology Press, 1993.

Keller, J. M., and Suzuki, K. "Use of the ARCS Motivation Model in Courseware Design." In D. H. Jonassen (ed.), *Instructional Designs for Microcomputer Courseware.* Hillsdale, N.J.: Erlbaum, 1988.

Means, T. B., Jonassen, D. H., and Dwyer, F. M. "Enhancing Relevance: Embedded ARCS Strategies Versus Purpose." *Educational Technology Research and Development,* 1997, 45 (1), 5–18.

Small, R. V., and Gluck, M. "The Relationship of Motivational Conditions to Effective Instructional Attributes: A Magnitude Scaling Approach." *Educational Technology,* 1994, 34 (8), 33–40.

Song, S. H. "The Effects of Motivationally Adaptive Computer-Assisted Instruction Developed Through the ARCS Model." Unpublished doctoral dissertation, College of Education, Florida State University, Tallahassee, Fla., 1998.

Suzuki, K., and Keller, J. M. "Creation and Cross-Cultural Validation of an ARCS Motivational Design Matrix." Paper presented at the annual meeting of the Japanese Association for Educational Technology, Kanazawa, Japan, 1996.

Visser, J., and Keller, J. M. "The Clinical Use of Motivational Messages: An Inquiry into the Validity of the ARCS Model of Motivational Design." *Instructional Science,* 1990, 19, 467–500.

Visser, L. "The Development of Motivational Communication in Distance Education Support." Unpublished doctoral dissertation, Educational Technology Department, University of Twente, the Netherlands, 1998.

JOHN M. KELLER is professor of education at Florida State University.

Problem-based learning requires strong student motivation. What elements of motivation are important when students learn through working out solutions to problems?

CORE Elements of Student Motivation in Problem-Based Learning

Marjorie M. MacKinnon

Few approaches to teaching and learning are more contingent upon student motivation than problem-based learning (PBL). Imagine, for example, that students are told, "Here's a toaster that isn't working. Fix it! Or better still, improve it" (Woods, 1994, p. 2.1). Given that students have little preparation for the task at hand, how are they to respond? Will they seem confused, shocked? According to Woods, the transition to PBL can be likened to the grieving process in that students often experience strong emotions, denial, and resistance before they accept, struggle, and eventually gain a sense of direction and integration.

PBL was developed in North America almost thirty years ago to prepare medical students for the realities of clinical practice (Barrows, 1996). In recent years, its application has been extended to many disciplines around the world (see, for example, Eitel and Gijselaers, 1997). Educators, particularly in professional programs, praise PBL for stimulating students to be highly motivated, self-directed learners who can integrate knowledge across subjects, reason critically, and work collaboratively with others (Barrows, 1996; Stokes, MacKinnon, and Whitehill, 1997).

In this chapter I share with readers what my colleagues and I are learning about student motivation based on a program of research being conducted at the University of Hong Kong. The data were obtained from thirty-six first-year undergraduate students (all Cantonese) who were asked to keep learning journals during their first exposure to PBL. In addition, presemester and postsemester measures were taken of their learning style preferences, and evaluations of the course by both students and teachers were compared with departmental norms.

Results (Stokes, MacKinnon, and Whitehill, 1997) showed that by the end of the semester students' learning preferences had significantly changed from teacher-dependent approaches to more active, independent formats. Students also rated the PBL course more favorably than they rated their other courses, and 88 percent indicated that they would take a similar course. In terms of academic achievement, students' case reports and exam performance were significantly higher in classes taught by the same faculty in all previous years (S. Stokes, personal communication, June 16, 1998). At the same time, however, the transition to PBL was not easy. Throughout the semester, learners reported strong feelings of fear, frustration, stress, confusion, and despair (Whitehill, Stokes, and MacKinnon, 1997). Because their initiation was so difficult, we wondered why students persisted and why they rated the course so favorably.

What Is PBL?

As its name suggests, PBL emphasizes learning (mastery) goals. Its aim is to develop self-directed, reflective, lifelong learners who can integrate knowledge, think critically, and work collaboratively with others (Barrows, 1988, 1996). The problems used should reflect important common situations that require integration of knowledge. In this way, relevance is used to provide the impetus for learning, and problems provide the framework for organizing and constructing knowledge (Gijselaers, 1996).

The structure of PBL is deceptively simple: students are presented with a complex, ill-structured problem that they are expected to resolve. Working in groups, they must generate hypotheses and questions about the problem, identify learning issues (that is, what they need to know in order to understand and solve the problem), and manage their workload fairly and efficiently. After each task or problem, groupmates are expected to evaluate their own performance and give honest, constructive feedback to one another (Barrows, 1988).

PBL contains many important elements for promoting intrinsic motivation for learning. As Dweck (1989) notes, when learning goals are emphasized, students become involved with learning for its own sake; they are more likely to take risks, admit ignorance, and persist at difficult tasks. However, much of the literature on achievement motivation was derived from experimental laboratory conditions and less is known about how students respond over extended periods when the level of challenge is high and when they are responsible for managing their own learning.

Hong Kong Students

Prior to piloting the course, it was difficult to predict how Hong Kong students would respond to PBL. Although Chinese learners tend to be high achievers who outperform their Western counterparts on examinations (Salili, 1996), university teachers often complain that students expect to be not only spoon-fed but also force-fed. Faculty often feel compelled to meet students' requests for detailed handouts, lecture notes, model essays, and prior exams. Although concrete materials may be important for students who are learning in a second language, the downside is that students continue to rely on memorization to perform well academically.

Some educators (for example, Biggs, 1996) argue that Hong Kong students' receptive learning style is largely due to the country's highly competitive educational system, which uses norm-referenced evaluations to streamline students and determine university placement (Tang and Biggs, 1996). The consequence of this performance-oriented system is that by the time students reach the university, many have experienced only didactic lectures and knowledge-based examinations.

The Course

The students in this study were in their second semester of a four-year professional degree program in speech and hearing sciences. The PBL course, Introduction to Communication Disorders, was imbedded within a traditional lecture-based curriculum and represented students' first exposure to the clinical aspects of speech therapy (speech-language pathology).

Task Structure. The coursework consisted of three parts: a three-hour orientation session and two problems, each lasting five weeks. Students divided into six groups and were provided with their own study room while two tutors monitored three groups each. (Following common practice, the term *tutor* is used throughout the remainder of this chapter to refer to faculty or instructors in this particular PBL role.) Tutors ran an orientation session to prepare students for the PBL process and provided written guidelines based on Woods (1994) for roles (manager, checker, recorder, and so on) so that learners could better maintain group functioning.

The Problems. The two problems were selected from actual clinical cases (one pediatric, one adult) to illustrate a range of speech-language difficulties and to stimulate integration of knowledge from subjects such as linguistics, anatomy and physiology, and psychology. For each problem, students were given a brief case description and shown a video of the patient interacting with a clinician.

Assessment. The content objectives for the course were to have students begin to identify internal and external influences that could have impacts on human communication and to suggest relevant treatment approaches. The process objectives were for students to identify, monitor, and evaluate aspects of their own learning. Students' performance was assessed in the following manner: groups submitted two case reports in which they described their diagnosis and treatment plans and how their plans were derived, and students had a final three-hour written examination. In addition, students were asked to keep an ungraded personal learning journal.

The CORE Elements

A total of 362 journal entries were analyzed in two stages. First, exploratory analysis was performed by having three investigators independently review the data in order to address the question, "What stands out?" (see Stokes, MacKinnon, and Whitehill, 1997). It was at this point that four themes or elements were noted: community, ownership, relevance, and empowerment (the CORE elements). In stage two of the study, frequency counts were performed on a weekly basis to verify the accuracy of our initial impressions.

As depicted in Figure 5.1, the results show that each of the four CORE elements strongly contributed to students' desire to learn and to work together enthusiastically. More important, we discovered that these CORE elements are not only interrelated but also synergetic; that is, the elements compensate for one another during difficult periods as well as strengthen and enrich one another during productive periods. In the following sections, the findings are discussed in relation to the literature on student motivation. To retain the spirit of students' comments, the quotations have not been edited.

Community. I use the term *community* to encapsulate teacher-student and student-student relationships because both contribute to students' per-

Figure 5.1. Differences in the Mean Proportion of Journal Entries that Discussed Community, Ownership, Relevance, and Empowerment During the Orientation, Case 1 and Case 2

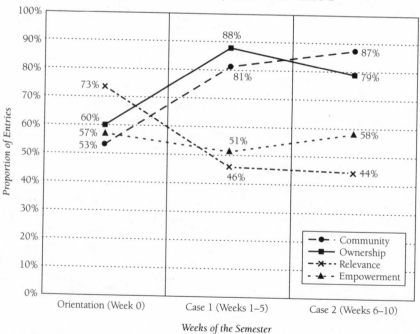

ceptions of classroom climate and to their sense of belonging. Eighty-one percent of the entries referred to the tutors, classmates, or both, suggesting that the social dimension of learning (community) was a critical aspect of students' learning experience.

Teacher-student relationships. Tutors played two important roles in promoting students' motivation for learning. First, they were energizers; they provided an orientation on the first day of class to heighten interest and introduce the PBL process. Students completed a Learning Preferences Inventory (Woods, 1994) and their scores were discussed in class. This helped students to see the link between their preferred learning styles (such as reading or discussion) and the PBL format. Tutors created a positive atmosphere for learning, using humor and a game (logic puzzle) to illustrate and practice the problem-solving strategies. As one student explained, "During the lecture, we were instructed to solve a detective problem. . . . We had no idea even after reading the case for several times. However, through discussion, we got more and more clues. And I realised that interacting with others does help learning a lot. We can gather different opinions from different persons" (17.0). As these comments illustrate, engendering a sense of competence is perhaps one of the most effective ways to create a positive disposition for learning (Bandura, 1986).

Once the PBL sessions began, the tutors' role was primarily facilitative and supportive, involving meeting with their groups to check on progress and to guide students' investigation by questioning their reasoning and raising issues that students had not considered. Facilitation was usually indirect so that learners were helped rather than led. Moreover, when students' progress was slow, the tutors provided moral support and encouragement, which inspired students to continue. "We are very happy that our facilitator appreciated what we've found out. This gave us encouragement to work on. Sometimes, I think we're just like small children. We always like to praised by others" (29.8). This comment is noteworthy because the tutor's intervention was seen as supportive rather than controlling. Studies have shown that when praise is noncontrolling, interest and persistence tend to remain high (Ames, 1992; Deci, 1995).

Student-student relationships. Students also showed marked differences in group development. In "high octane" groups, where members were already friends, students had fun. They would joke, dance, or dim the lights to create a relaxed atmosphere; yet they were intellectually aggressive and eager to participate. As noted by Dweck (1989), having fun is compatible with the pursuit of learning goals because the attractiveness of the learning method is enhanced.

For the majority of groups, students were less familiar with each other, more serious initially, and less confident or proactive. They benefited from having guidelines for rotating assigned roles (Woods, 1994) because the structure helped to alleviate learners' anxiety. Many students were remarkably diligent about performing their roles because they saw them as important for group functioning and because they could use the skills (such as chairing meetings) in a variety of situations.

Though students were often unsupervised, they were very task oriented. One explanation is that students felt an obligation to the group (Paris and Turner, 1994). Our data indicate that students' commitment went far beyond simple feelings of duty or obligation. Instead, their sense of community was a powerful source of motivation (Whitehill, Stokes, and MacKinnon, 1997). "We are working to our limit, yet without any reluctance—through cooperation, all our group members have developed deep friendship, sense of trust and confidence. This is very precious. . . . I think I have improved a bit my weakness— slowness. This is FORCED to improve, really, since I am in such an efficient team, that the shame will drive me to craziness if I can't finish work on time" (30.14).

Further analysis revealed that the combination of a salient goal (relevant content) and a heavy workload were the factors that contributed most to building a sense of community. Each week students returned from self-study to share their "treasures" (what some students called the information they found) with groupmates. Through the process of sharing knowledge and discussing concepts, deep emotional bonds developed, because students' contributions and hard work were truly appreciated. As Ames (1992, p. 263) concludes, "A sense of belonging . . . represents an integration of self with task and others."

Ownership. One of the most important features of PBL is the combination of autonomy and ownership. Eighty-two percent of students' entries were related to issues of ownership (MacKinnon, 1998) and personal control of learning. Students used the active voice when describing their role in the division of labor ("Today I was the chair"), their goals for the session ("We wanted to look at. . . ."), the tasks they completed ("We screened out irrelevant hypotheses"), and their sense of accomplishment and satisfaction ("We are solving the problems ourselves"). This suggests that learners adopted an internal locus of responsibility (Ames, 1992).

Another factor that contributed to students' sense of autonomy was related to their interactions with the tutors. In PBL, when groups encounter difficulty, it is their responsibility to try to resolve it (Barrows, 1988). It is a mistake for tutors to come to the rescue, because this would imply that students are not competent. As Deci (1995) warns, this will undermine students' autonomy and their intrinsic motivation will drain away.

On a few occasions, the tutors broke with the PBL tradition and provided direct assistance. Their interventions included showing students how to map ideas, demonstrating symptoms (slurred speech), and suggesting key words to investigate (such as *anomia*). Because students could not gain such information on their own, these interventions were appreciated, yet they preserved students' sense of autonomy and self-efficacy. At the end of the course, students' final entries often expressed thanks to the tutors for their "great help" and "enlightenment." They also described the teachers as friendly, concerned, and supportive. I believe that these impressions were based on the tutors' willingness to respond to students' needs while maintaining the students' autonomy.

Relevance. In PBL, problem relevance is considered the most important factor for motivation and for developing clinical reasoning skills (Barrows, 1986). In our sample, 48 percent of the journal entries contained comments about the relevance of the course, the content, the PBL learning method, or some combination of the three. Although this figure is less than the number of times community and ownership were mentioned (81 and 82 percent, respectively), qualitative analysis (Whitehill, Stokes, and MacKinnon, 1997) indicated that relevance may have played a vital role in intrinsic motivation. The following comment was made after the PBL orientation session: "Today's class really excite me. It was the first time I can clearly tell myself that I'm studying Speech and Hearing Sciences. It may sound funny but it's true. Last semester, I have to learn many things but they just kept me busy to understand them. I don't have the time to relate them to speech and hearing. Finally I get lost. I don't know why I'm doing such things. I get tired everyday. Working all through the day but without any goal. This made me suffer a lot" (10.0).

As illustrated here, when relevance was not apparent, learning became a joyless task and a test of fortitude. Moreover, busy work that had no apparent relevance was disempowering because it deprived students of a sense of ownership and self-determination.

Working with actual clinical cases was perceived as highly relevant to students' professional careers and they became personally invested in resolving each problem. When groups completed their report and saw a posttreatment video of their first client, they shared a sense of personal fulfillment and joy: "During the past five weeks, we have done a lot to assess and plan treatment for the child. We worked very hard for it. We came across many difficulties and frustration. It seems like we have actually involved in helping the child to communicate normally. So, happiness comes from the bottom of heart when we saw the progress of the child. This is the first time I gain satisfaction" (5.8).

The method of learning was also seen as relevant. Most students were happy to work in groups because they could learn transferable skills, such as how to chair meetings, find information, share and discuss findings, brainstorm, reason critically, deal with conflict, cooperate with others, set their own goals, and manage their time effectively. The relevance of these learning outcomes to other courses and to the students' future careers may help to explain the close link between relevance and empowerment.

Empowerment. The term *empowerment* has two connotations: to give authority or power to someone, and to gain power, strength, or competence. Within the classroom context, opportunities for challenge and mastery help to engender a sense of competence (Bandura, 1986; Ames, 1992). Mastery alone may not be enough, however, to maintain intrinsic motivation. As deCharms (1976) points out, without autonomy students learn only to be competent pawns. Empowerment therefore involves providing students with a sense of mastery in skills that they perceive as valuable (relevant) and attained through their own efforts.

In our sample, students seemed enthusiastic and acutely aware of what they were learning. In 54 percent of their journal entries, learners described gains in their confidence, attitudes, knowledge, and skills (MacKinnon, 1998). Two aspects of the course are worth noting. One is that groups recorded and reviewed their activities on a weekly basis. This gave them a sense of achievement and improved their ability and willingness to work as a team.

Having a second problem to address midway through the course provided students with a valuable benchmark for estimating their progress. The second time around, students found that they were no longer afraid or uncertain. They were comfortable working together and they knew how to organize and distribute their workload. Having a point of comparison enabled students to take pride in their accomplishments. The implication for faculty is to consider strategies that will enable students to see both the before and after pictures so that they recognize their learning needs and their accomplishments over time. "At first I was shocked by the totally new teaching/learning approach. I think that the PBL was not effective because I am get used to the traditional lectures. But after several discussions, I learn how to solve problems more systematically in both cases. During discussion, I learn to accept different opinions and cooperate with others. Listening to others and expressing our views can improve one interpersonal relationships. I am more initiative to prepare our discussion and find reference books. Moreover, PBL gives us a goal to achieve, this challenging and interesting task make us more active in learning" (32.14).

Conclusion

What should stand out from these findings is that community, ownership, relevance, and empowerment are synergetic. If any element is missing, it is likely that the motivational impact of the remaining elements will be somehow diminished. For example, if students do not perceive the relevance of the content, they may be less inclined to complete their work, which in turn will reduce their sense of community and empowerment. Likewise, if students work individually, only the teacher can appreciate their hard work. With reduced social support (community), we can anticipate that many students will be less inclined to exert such high levels of effort. Again, their sense of empowerment and their perceptions of relevance are likely to decline accordingly.

Although our findings are based on the experiences of one undergraduate cohort whose culture is richly Chinese (see Whitehill, Stokes, and Mac-Kinnon, 1997), these elements address our basic human needs for affinity, esteem, and self-actualization (Maslow, 1968; Rogers, 1967). This may explain why they appear to be at the very "CORE" of intrinsic motivation.

The implication for teachers, therefore, is to consider ways to include each element in their course designs and classroom interactions. One strategy is simply to ask oneself some very basic questions, such as, How can I build a sense of community in my classroom? Are there ways to ensure that students' contributions will be appreciated? How can I show them the before-and-after picture so that they feel their learning is relevant and empowering? The rest is a matter of careful attention, balance, and the willingness to let learners share leadership roles.

References

Ames, C. "Classrooms: Goals, Structures, and Student Motivation." *Journal of Educational Psychology,* 1992, *84* (3), 261–271.

Bandura, A. *Social Foundations of Thought and Action.* Englewood Cliffs, N.J.: Prentice Hall, 1986.

Barrows, H. S. "A Taxonomy of Problem-Based Learning Methods." *Medical Education,* 1986, *20,* 481–486.

Barrows, H. S. *The Tutorial Process.* Springfield: Southern Illinois University School of Medicine, 1988.

Barrows, H. S. "Problem-Based Learning in Medicine and Beyond: A Brief Overview." In L. Wilkerson and W. H. Gijselaers (eds.), *Bringing Problem-Based Learning to Higher Education: Theory and Practice.* New Directions for Teaching and Learning, no. 68. San Francisco: Jossey-Bass, 1996.

Biggs, J. "Western Misconceptions of the Confucian-Heritage Learning Culture." In D. Watkins and J. Biggs (eds.), *The Chinese Learner: Cultural, Psychological and Contextual Influences.* Hong Kong: Comparative Education Research Centre and the Australian Council for Educational Research Ltd., 1996.

deCharms, R. *Enhancing Motivation: Change in the Classroom.* New York: Irvington, 1976.

Deci, E. *Why We Do What We Do: The Dynamics of Personal Autonomy.* New York: Putnam, 1995.

Dweck, C. "Motivation." In A. Lesgold and R. Glaser (eds.), *Foundations for a Psychology of Education.* Hillsdale, N.J.: Erlbaum, 1989.

Eitel, F., and Gijselaers, W. (eds.). "Problem-Based Learning: Theory, Practice, and Research." *Zeitschrift für Hochschuldidaktik* [Journal of University Didactics], 1997, *2* (1).

Gijselaers, W. "Connecting Problem-Based Practices with Educational Theory." In L. Wilkerson and W. H. Gijselaers (eds.), *Bringing Problem-Based Learning to Higher Education: Theory and Practice.* New Directions for Teaching and Learning, no. 68. San Francisco: Jossey-Bass, 1996.

MacKinnon, M. "Achievement Motivation: Lessons Learned from Hong Kong Students." Paper presented at the International Conference on the Application of Psychology to the Quality of Learning and Teaching, Hong Kong, June 13, 1998.

Maslow, A. *Toward a Psychology of Being.* (2nd ed.) New York: Van Nostrand Reinhold, 1968.

Paris, S., and Turner, J. "Situated Motivation." In P. Pintrich, D. Brown, and C. Weinstein (eds.), *Student Motivation, Cognition, and Learning.* Hillsdale, N.J.: Erlbaum, 1994.

Rogers, C. *On Becoming a Person: A Therapist's View of Psychotherapy.* London: Constable, 1967.

Salili, F. "Accepting Personal Responsibility for Learning." In D. Watkins and J. Biggs (eds.), *The Chinese Learner: Cultural, Psychological and Contextual Influences.* Hong Kong: Comparative Education Research Centre and the Australian Council for Educational Research Ltd., 1996.

Stokes, S., MacKinnon, M., and Whitehill, T. "Students' Experiences of PBL: Journal and Questionnaire Analysis." *Zeitschrift für Hochschuldidaktik* [Journal of University Didactics], 1997, *21* (1), 161–179.

Tang, C., and Biggs, J. "How Hong Kong Students Cope with Assessment." In D. Watkins and J. Biggs (eds.), *The Chinese Learner: Cultural, Psychological and Contextual Influences.* Hong Kong: Comparative Education Research Centre and the Australian Council for Educational Research Ltd., 1996.

Whitehill, T., Stokes, S., and MacKinnon, M. "Problem-Based Learning and the Chinese Learner." In R. Murray-Harvey and H. Silins (eds.), *Learning and Teaching in Higher Education: Advancing International Perspectives.* Adelaide, Australia: Flinders Press, 1997.

Woods, D. *Problem-Based Learning: How to Gain the Most from PBL.* Waterdown, Canada: Woods, 1994.

MARJORIE M. MACKINNON is associate professor at the Centre for the Advancement of University Teaching at the University of Hong Kong.

Cooperative learning (CL) is an instructional strategy that employs a variety of motivational techniques to make instruction more relevant and students more responsible. This chapter outlines the benefits of CL in terms of its motivational impact.

The Motivational Benefits of Cooperative Learning

Theodore Panitz

General guidelines for classroom motivation (for example, Forsyth and McMillan, 1994) suggest emphasis on challenging, engaging, informative activities and the building of enthusiasm and a sense of responsibility in learners. Well-developed instructional strategies such as cooperative learning (CL) offer many potential benefits to learners (Panitz, 1998).

The definition of CL as a motivational strategy includes all learning situations in which students work in groups to accomplish particular learning objectives and in which they are interdependent for successful completion of the objective. Forsyth and McMillan (1991) emphasize intrinsic motivation as a key element in teaching and learning, as does Wlodkowski (see Chapter One of this issue), noting that successful intrinsic motivation develops attitude, establishes inclusion, engenders competence, and enhances meaning within diverse students. How can CL be a positive motivator for a diverse student population? This chapter attempts to answer that question.

DEVELOPING ATTITUDE: *Creating a favorable disposition toward the learning experience through personal relevance and choice*

A primary benefit of CL is that it enhances students' self-esteem, which in turn motivates students to participate in the learning process (Johnson and Johnson, 1989). Cooperative efforts among students result in a higher degree of accomplishment by all participants (Slavin, 1987). Students help one another and in doing so build a supportive community that raises the performance level of each member (Kagan, 1986). This in turn leads to higher self-esteem in all students (Webb, 1982).

NEW DIRECTIONS FOR TEACHING AND LEARNING, no. 78, Summer 1999 © Jossey-Bass Publishers

Cooperation enhances student satisfaction with the learning experience by actively involving students in designing and completing class procedures and course content (Johnson and Johnson, 1990). Effective teams or groups assume ownership of a process and its results when individuals are encouraged to work together toward a common goal, often defined by the group. This aspect is especially helpful for individuals who have a history or failure (Turnure and Zigler, 1958).

CL promotes mastery while passive acceptance of information from an outside expert often promotes a sense of helplessness and reliance on others to grasp concepts. In a typical college classroom that emphasizes lecturing there is little time for reflection and discussion of students' errors or misconceptions. In the CL paradigm, students are continuously discussing, debating, and clarifying their understanding of the concepts.

CL reduces classroom anxiety created by new and unfamiliar situations faced by students (Kessler, Price, and Wortman, 1985). In a traditional classroom, when a teacher calls on a student, that student becomes the focus of attention of the entire class. Any mistakes or incorrect answers become subject to scrutiny by the whole class. In contrast, in a CL situation when students work in a group, the focus of attention is diffused among the group. In addition, the group produces a product that its members can review prior to presenting it to the whole class, thus diminishing prospects that mistakes will occur at all (Slavin and Karweit, 1981). When a mistake is made, it becomes a teaching tool instead of a public criticism of an individual student.

In CL, test anxiety is significantly reduced (Johnson and Johnson, 1989). CL provides many opportunities for alternate forms of student assessment (Panitz and Panitz, 1996). This leads to a reduction in test anxiety because the students see that the teacher is able to evaluate how they think as well as what they know. Through interactions with students during each class, the teacher gains a better understanding of each student's learning style and how each student performs, and an opportunity is created whereby the teacher may provide extra guidance and counseling for the students.

CL develops positive student-teacher attitudes (Johnson and Johnson, 1989). The level of involvement of all the participants in a cooperative system is very intense and personal. Teachers learn about student behaviors because students have many opportunities to explain their actions and thoughts to the teacher. Lines of communication are opened and actively encouraged. Teachers have more opportunities to explain why policies are established, and the system allows students to have more input into establishing policies and class procedures. The empowerment created by the many interpersonal interactions leads to a very positive attitude on the part of all parties involved.

CL sets high expectations for students and teachers (Panitz and Panitz, 1998). Being made responsible for one's learning and for one's peers presumes that one has that capability. By setting obtainable goals for groups and by facilitating group interaction, teachers establish high expectations that become self-fulfilling as the students master the cooperative approach, learn how to work well together in teams, and demonstrate their abilities through a variety of assessment methods.

CL establishes inclusion, creating a learning atmosphere in which learners feel respected and connected to one another. It creates a strong social support system (Cohen and Willis, 1985). CL techniques use students' social experiences in such activities as warm-up exercises and group-building activities to encourage their involvement in the learning process. The teacher plays an active role in facilitating the process by interacting with each student while moving around the class and observing students interacting (Cooper and others, 1985). Teachers may raise questions with individuals or small groups to help advise students or explain concepts. In addition, a natural tendency to socialize with the students on a professional level is created. Students often mention offhandedly that they are having difficulties outside of class related to work, family, friends, and so on. Openings like this can lead to discussion of those problems by the teacher and student in a nonthreatening way due to the informality of the situation, and additional support from other student services units in such areas can be a beneficial by-product (Kessler and McCleod, 1985).

CL develops students' social interaction skills. A major component of learning elaborated by Johnson, Johnson, and Holubec (1984) includes training students in the social skills needed to work cooperatively. In our society and current educational framework, competition is valued over cooperation. By asking group members to identify what behaviors help them work together and by asking individuals to reflect on their contribution to the group's success or failure, students are made aware of the need for healthy, positive, helping interactions (Panitz, 1996; Cohen and Cohen, 1991).

According to Kessler and McCleod (1985), "CL promotes positive societal responses . . . reduces violence in any setting . . . eliminates fear and blame, and increases honor, friendliness, and consensus. Process is as important as content and goal. CL takes time to master, and facilitators who have done the personal work that allows sharing of power, service to the learners, and natural learning find CL a joy" (p. 219).

Sherman (1991) makes the observation that "most social psychology text books contain considerable discussions about conflict and its resolution or reduction. Almost all introductory educational psychology text books now contain extended discussions of effective pedagogies for improving racial relations, self-esteem, internal locus of control, and academic achievement" (Messick and Mackie, 1989).

CL fosters student interaction at all levels (Webb, 1982). Research has shown that when students of high ability work with students of lower ability, the former benefit by explaining or demonstrating and the latter benefit by seeing an approach to problem solving modeled by a peer (Johnson and Johnson, 1985; Swing and Peterson, 1982; Hooper and Hannafin, 1988). Warm-up and group-building activities help students to understand their differences and to learn how to capitalize on them rather than use them as a basis for antagonism.

CL helps majority and minority populations in a class learn to work with each other (R. M. Felder, personal e-mail communication, 1997; Johnson and Johnson, 1972; Slavin, 1980). Because students are actively involved in exploring issues and interacting with each other on a regular basis in a guided fashion, they are able to understand their differences and learn how to resolve social problems that may arise (Johnson and Johnson, 1985). Training students in conflict resolution is a major component of collaborative learning (Aronson and others, 1978; Slavin, 1987).

CL establishes an atmosphere of cooperation and helping schoolwide (Deutsch, 1975). CL focuses attention on the accomplishments of the group as well as the individual. Teamwork is the modus operandi and intergroup cooperation is encouraged. Even when group competitions are used (Slavin, 1987), the intent is to create a positive helping environment for all participants. In CL environments, students are taught how to criticize ideas, not people (Johnson, Johnson, and Holubec, 1984). A function of CL is to help students resolve differences amicably. They need to be taught how to challenge ideas and advocate for their positions without personalizing their statements. In cooperative classes, students may be assigned roles in order to build interdependence within the groups. These roles often model societal and work-related roles that students will encounter in real life. Adult motivational theory has shown that the direct applicability of classroom small-group problem solving to students' lives will enhance motivation to learn (Wlodkowski, 1985).

CL is particularly effective at increasing the leadership skills of female students and at getting male students used to turning to women for help in pressure situations (Bean, 1996). This benefit is especially important in mathematics classes, where men generally dominate class discussions and presentations. Johnson and Johnson (1990) point out that "students tend to like and enjoy math more and be more intrinsically motivated to learn more about it continually" (p. 121). CL also helps to develop learning communities within classes and institutions (Tinto, 1997). Community colleges and many four-year colleges are primarily commuter schools. Students do not remain on campus for extracurricular or social activities. Many students have jobs, family pressures, or both, which also limits their ability to participate in campus life. Thus it falls to the classroom teacher to create an atmosphere of community within the college. The previous discussion of the social benefits of CL makes it clear that creating a community of learners is easily accomplished using CL techniques. There is a significant benefit to CL that is not always apparent because it takes place outside of the classroom. If groups operate long enough during a course, the people in them will get to know each other and extend their activities outside of class. Students will exchange phone numbers and contact each other to get help with questions or problems they are having, and they will often sign up together for classes in later terms and seek out teachers who use CL methods (Bean, 1996; R. M. Felder, personal e-mail communication, 1997).

ENGENDERING COMPETENCE: *Creating an understanding that learners are effective in learning something they value*

CL develops higher level thinking skills (Webb, 1982). Students are engaged in the learning process instead of passively listening to the teacher. Pairs of students (followed by threesomes and larger groups) working together represent the most effective form of interaction (Schwartz, Black, and Strange, 1991). When students work in pairs, one person is listening while the other person is discussing the question under investigation. Both are developing valuable problem-solving skills by formulating their ideas, discussing them, receiving immediate feedback, and responding to questions and comments (Johnson, 1971; Peterson and Swing, 1985). This aspect of CL does not preclude whole class discussion. In fact, whole class discussion is enhanced by having students think out and discuss ideas thoroughly before the entire class discusses an idea or concept. In addition, the teacher may temporarily join a group's discussion to question ideas or statements made by group members or to clarify concepts or questions raised by students.

CL fosters higher levels of performance (Bligh, 1972). Critical thinking skills increase and retention of information and interest in the subject matter improve (Kulik and Kulik, 1979). This creates a positive cycle of good performance, building higher self-esteem, which in turn leads to more interest in the subject and better performance (Keller, 1983). Students share their success with their groups, thus enhancing both the individual's and the group's self-esteem.

Skill building and practice can be enhanced and made less tedious through CL activities used both in and out of class (Tannenberg, 1995). To develop critical thinking skills, students need a base of information from which to work. Acquiring this base often requires some degree of repetition and memory work. When this is accomplished individually, the process can be tedious, boring, or overwhelming. When students work together, the learning process becomes interesting and fun despite the repetitive nature of the learning process. Male (1990), for example, has documented the positive impact of CL in drill-and-practice computer use.

CL develops students' oral communication skills (Yager, Johnson, and Johnson, 1985). When students work in pairs, one partner verbalizes his or her idea while the other listens, asks questions, or comments on what she or he has heard. Clarification and explanation of one's ideas is a very important part of the cooperative process and requires higher-order thinking skills (Johnson, Johnson, Roy, and Zaidman, 1985). Students who tutor each other must develop a clear idea of the concept they are presenting and orally communicate it to their partner (Neer, 1987).

ENHANCING MEANING: *Creating challenging, thoughtful learning experiences that include learners' values and perspectives and contribute to an equitable society*

The focus of CL is to involve students actively in the learning process (Slavin, 1980). Whenever two or more students attempt to solve a problem or answer a question, they become involved in the process of exploratory learning. Promotive interaction, a basic principle of CL, builds students' sense of responsibility to themselves and their group members through reliance on one another's talents, and CL assessment processes reward both individuals and groups, thus reinforcing this interdependence (Baird and White, 1984).

During the cooperative process, students can become involved in developing curricula and class procedures (Kort, 1992). They are often asked to assess themselves, their groups, and class procedures (Meier and Panitz, 1996). Teachers can take advantage of this immediate formative input without having to wait for the results of exams or course evaluations. Students who participate in structuring the class assume ownership of the process, and their opinions and observations are given credibility. CL helps students wean themselves from considering teachers as the sole sources of knowledge and understanding (R. M. Felder, personal e-mail communication, 1997).

The primary foci in CL are the process of learning and the means by which individuals function independently and within groups. The high level of interaction and interdependence among group members leads to "deep" rather than "surface" learning (Entwistle and Tait, 1994), and to more emphasis on higher-order learning (see Donald, Chapter Three in this issue). CL is student centered, leading to an emphasis on learning as well as teaching and to more student ownership of responsibility for that learning. In contrast, other teaching paradigms consist of individual student effort, competitive testing to assess competence, and an evaluation hierarchy based on "grade orientation" rather than "learning orientation" (Lowman, 1987).

Students who develop personal professional relations with teachers by getting to know them and who work on projects outside of class achieve better results and tend to stay in school (Cooper, 1994; Hagman and Hayes, 1986). Teachers who get to know their students get to understand their learning styles and problems and can often find ways of dealing with those problems and inspiring students (Janke, 1980). According to Felder (personal e-mail communication, 1997), additional benefits accrue to students in grade improvement, retention of information, information transfer to other courses and disciplines, and improved class attendance. There is a strong positive correlation between class attendance and success in courses (Johnson and Johnson, 1989), which may help account for the improved performance.

Students who are involved in the learning process are much more likely to become interested in learning and to make an effort to attend school (Astin, 1977). A class in which students interact fosters an environment conducive to high student motivation, participation, and attendance (Treisman, 1983, 1992).

CL inherently calls for self-management by students (Resnick, 1987). To function within their groups, students are trained to come prepared, with assignments completed and an understanding of the material they are going to contribute to their group. They are also given time to process group behaviors, such as checking with one another to make sure that homework assignments are not only completed but understood. These promotive interactions help students learn self-management techniques.

CL increases students' persistence and the likelihood of successful completion of assignments (R. M. Felder, personal e-mail communication, 1997). When individuals get stuck they are more likely to give up, but groups are much more likely to find ways to keep going. This concept is reinforced by Johnson and Johnson (1990), who state, "In a learning situation, student goal achievements are positively correlated; students perceive that they can reach learning goals if and only if the other students in the learning group also reach their goals. Thus, students seek outcomes that are beneficial to all those with whom they are cooperatively linked" (p. 121).

CL provides many advantages to teachers and learners. Many of these advantages arise from the intrinsic motivational strengths of CL and the extent to which CL fosters student interest, behavioral and attitudinal change, and opportunities for success. As Keller (1983) demonstrates, this set of outcomes results from the successful incorporation of motivational issues into instruction.

References

Aronson, E., Blaney, N., Stephan, C., Sikes, J., and Snapp, M. "The Jigsaw Classroom." Thousand Oaks, Calif.: Sage, 1978.

Astin, A. W. *Four Critical Years: Effects of College Beliefs, Attitudes, and Knowledge.* San Francisco: Jossey-Bass, 1977.

Baird, J., and White, R. "Improving Learning Through Enhanced Metacognition: A Classroom Study." Paper presented at the annual meeting of the American Educational Research Association, New Orleans, Apr. 23–27, 1984.

Bean, J. *Engaging Ideas: The Professor's Guide to Integrating Writing, Critical Thinking, and Active Learning in the Classroom.* San Francisco: Jossey-Bass, 1996.

Bligh, D. A. *What's the Use of Lectures?* Harmondsworth, England: Penguin, 1972.

Cohen, B. P., and Cohen, E. G. "From Groupwork Among Children to R&D Teams: Interdependence, Interaction and Productivity." In E. J. Lawler (ed.), *Advances in Group Processes.* Vol. 8. Greenwich, Conn.: JAI Press, 1991.

Cohen, S., and Willis, T. "Stress and Social Support and the Buffering Hypothesis." *Psychological Bulletin,* 1985, *98,* 310–357.

Cooper, C. "Coming of Age." *Cooperative Learning,* 1994, *12* (2), 3–5.

Cooper, J., Prescott, S., Cook, L., Smith, L., Mueck, R., and Cuseo, J. *Cooperative Learning and College Instruction: Effective Use of Student Learning Teams.* Sacramento: California State Foundation, 1985.

Deutsch, M. "Equity, Equality and Need: What Determines Which Value Will Be Used as the Basis of Distributive Justice." *Journal of Social Issues,* 1975, *31,* 137–149.

Entwistle, N., and Tait, H. "Approaches to Studying and Preferences for Teaching in Higher Education: Implications for Student Ratings." *Instructional Evaluation and Faculty Development,* 1994, *14* (1–2), 2–9.

Forsyth, D. R., and McMillan, J. H. "Practical Proposals for Motivating Students." In R. J. Menges and M. D. Svinicki (eds.), *College Teaching: From Theory to Practice.* New Directions for Teaching and Learning, no. 45. San Francisco: Jossey Bass, 1991.

Hagman, J., and Hayes, J. *Cooperative Learning: Effects of Task, Reward, and Group Size on Individual Achievement.* Technical Report no. 704. Alexandria, Va.: U.S. Army Research Institute for the Behavioral Sciences, 1986. (ED 278 720)

Hooper, S., and Hannafin, M. J. "Cooperative CBI: The Effects of Heterogeneous Versus Homogeneous Grouping on the Learning of Progressively Complex Concepts." *Journal of Educational Computing Research,* 1988, *4,* 413–424.

Janke, R. "Computational Errors of Mentally Retarded Students." *Psychology in the Schools,* 1980, *17,* 30–32.

Johnson, D. W. "Communication and the Inducement of Cooperative Behavior in Conflicts: A Critical Review." *Speech Monographs,* 1971, *41,* 64–78.

Johnson, D. W., Johnson, R. T., and Holubec, E. J. *Cooperation in the Classroom.* Edina, Minn.: Interaction, 1984.

Johnson, D. W., Johnson, R. T., Roy, P., and Zaidman, B. "Oral Interaction in Cooperative Learning Groups: Speaking, Listening and the Nature of Statements Made by High-, Medium- and Low-Achieving Students." *Journal of Psychology,* 1985, *119,* 303–321.

Johnson, R. T., and Johnson, D. W. "The Effects of Others' Actions, Attitude Similarity, and Race on Attraction Toward Others." *Human Relations,* 1972, *25* (2), 121–130.

Johnson, R. T., and Johnson, D. W. "Relationships Between Black and White Students in Intergroup Cooperation and Competition." *Journal of Social Psychology,* 1985, *125* (4), 421–428.

Johnson, R. T., and Johnson, D. W. "Cooperation and Competition Theory and Research." Edina, Minn.: Interaction, 1989.

Johnson, R. T., and Johnson, D. W. "Using Cooperative Learning in Math." In N. Davidson (ed.), *Cooperative Learning in Mathematics.* Menlo Park, Calif.: Addison-Wesley, 1990.

Kagan, S. "Cooperative Learning and Sociological Factors in Schooling." In C. Cortes (ed.), *Beyond Language: Social and Cultural Factors in Schooling Language-Minority Students.* Los Angeles: California State University Evaluation, Dissemination and Assessment Center, 1986.

Keller, J. M. "Motivational Design of Instruction." In C. M. Reigeluth (ed.), *Instructional Design Theories and Models: An Overview of Their Current Status.* Hillsdale, N.J.: Erlbaum, 1983.

Kessler, R., and McCleod, J. "Social Support and Mental Health in Community Samples." In S. Cohen and S. L. Syme (eds.), *Social Support and Health.* Orlando, Fla.: Academic Press, 1985.

Kessler, R., Price, R., and Wortman, C. "Social Factors in Psychopathology: Stress, Social Support and Coping Processes." *Annual Review of Psychology,* 1985, *36,* 351–372.

Kort, M. S. "Down from the Podium." In K. Kroll (ed.), *Maintaining Faculty Excellence.* New Directions for Community Colleges, no. 79. San Francisco: Jossey-Bass, 1992.

Kulik, J. A., and Kulik, C. L. "College Teaching." In P. Peterson and H. Walberg (eds.), *Research in Teaching: Concepts, Findings and Implications.* Berkeley, Calif.: McCutchan, 1979.

Lowman, J. "Testing Issues in Large Classes." In M. G. Weimer (ed.), *Teaching Large Classes Well.* New Directions for Teaching and Learning, no. 32. San Francisco: Jossey-Bass, 1987.

Male, M. "Cooperative Learning and Computers in the Elementary and Middle School Math Classroom." In N. Davidson (ed.), *Cooperative Learning in Mathematics.* Menlo Park, Calif.: Addison-Wesley, 1990.

Meier, M., and Panitz, T. "Ending on a High Note: Better Endings for Classes and Courses." *College Teaching,* Fall 1996.

Messick, D. M., and Mackie, D. M. "Intergroup Relations." *Annual Review of Psychology,* 1989, *40,* 45–81.

Neer, M. R. "The Development of an Instrument to Measure Classroom Apprehension." *Communication Education,* 1987, *36,* 154–166.

Panitz, T. "Getting Students Ready for Learning." *Cooperative Learning and College Teaching,* 1996, *6* (2), 7–10.

Panitz, T. "Benefits of Collaborative Learning." Posting to the listserv of the Professional and Organizational Development Network (pod@iastate.edu), Apr. 22, 1998.

Panitz, T., and Panitz, P. "Assessing Students and Yourself by Observing Students Working Cooperatively and Using the One-Minute Paper." *Cooperative Learning and College Teaching,* 1996, *6* (3), 14.

Panitz, T., and Panitz, P. "Encouraging the Use of Collaborative Learning in Higher Education." In J. J. Forest (ed.), *Issues Facing International Education.* New York: Garland, 1998.

Peterson, P., and Swing, S. "Students' Cognitions as Mediators of the Effectiveness of Small-Group Learning." *Journal of Educational Psychology,* 1985, *77* (3), 299–312.

Resnick, L. B. "Education and Learning to Think." Washington, D.C.: National Academy Press, 1987.

Schwartz, D. L., Black, J. B., and Strange, J. "Dyads Have Fourfold Advantage over Individuals Inducing Abstract Rules." Paper presented at the annual meeting of the American Educational Research Association, Chicago, Apr. 1991.

Sherman, L. W. "Cooperative Learning in Post-Secondary Education: Implications from Social Psychology for Active Learning Experiences." Paper presented at the annual meeting of the American Educational Research Association, Chicago, Apr. 1991.

Slavin, R. E. "Cooperative Learning." *Review of Educational Research,* 1980, *50,* 315–342.

Slavin, R. E. "Cooperative Learning: Student Teams." (2nd ed.) Washington, D.C.: National Education Association, 1987.

Slavin, R. E., and Karweit, N. "Cognitive and Affective Outcomes of an Intensive Student Team Learning Experience." *Journal of Experimental Education,* 1981, *50,* 29–35.

Swing, S., and Peterson, P. "The Relationship of Student Ability and Small Group Interaction to Student Achievement." *American Educational Research Journal,* 1982, *19,* 259–274.

Tannenberg, J. "Using Cooperative Learning in the Undergraduate Computer Science Classroom." *Proceedings of the Midwest Small College Computing Conference,* 1995.

Tinto, V. "Enhancing Learning via Community." *Thought and Action: The NEA Higher Education Journal,* 1997, *6* (1), 53–54.

Treisman, U. "Improving the Performance of Minority Students in College Level Mathematics." *Innovation Abstracts,* June 1983, *5* (17).

Treisman, U. "Studying Students Studying Calculus: A Look at the Lives of Minority Students in College." *College Mathematics Journal,* 1992, *23* (5), 362–372.

Turnure, J., and Zigler, R. "Outer-Directedness in the Problem Solving of Normal and Retarded Students." *Journal of Abnormal and Social Psychology,* 1958, *57,* 379–388.

Webb, N. M. "Group Composition, Group Interaction, and Achievement in Small Groups." *Journal of Educational Psychology,* 1982, *74* (4), 475–484.

Wlodkowski, R. J. *Enhancing Motivation to Learn.* San Francisco: Jossey-Bass, 1985.

Yager, S., Johnson, D. W., and Johnson, R. "Oral Discussion, Groups-to-Individual Transfer, and Achievement in Cooperative Learning Groups." *Journal of Educational Psychology,* 1985, *77* (1), 60–66.

THEODORE PANITZ is professor in the Department of Mathematics, Engineering, and Technology at Cape Cod Community College.

PART THREE

Motivation and the Institution

A supportive teaching culture constitutes a context that promotes the availability of various forms of informative feedback about an individual's teaching effectiveness, which in turn stimulates teachers' motivation for instructional excellence.

Faculty Motivation: The Role of a Supportive Teaching Culture

Kenneth A. Feldman, Michael B. Paulsen

College instructors are part of organizations whose cultures may have both positive and negative impacts on instructors' motivations. Recently we (Paulsen and Feldman, 1995a) described how researchers and practitioners have begun to develop a more refined appreciation of the content of one such culture— the teaching culture. In this chapter we briefly outline the significance of teaching cultures to faculty motivation and to excellence in teaching.

There has been a gradual shift over the past century toward a research model in American colleges and universities (Clark, 1987; Schuster and Bowen, 1985). Even so, the research culture is not necessarily the dominant culture at all colleges and universities. Regardless of whether the teaching culture is dominant or subordinate, the characteristics of a supportive teaching culture are of great importance. We assume that faculty motivation to teach, the maintenance of instructional excellence, and the effectiveness of strategies to improve instruction all clearly benefit by the presence of a culture that is supportive of teaching.

Characteristics of a Supportive Teaching Culture

The research literature—consisting primarily of qualitative studies, case studies, and surveys—has consistently identified a number of prominent characteristics of cultures that support teaching and its improvement. Eight of these characteristics are especially salient.

High-level administrative commitment and support. To maintain excellence in teaching or to promote faculty motivation and (when necessary) instructional improvement, the unambiguous commitment and support of senior administrators is especially important. When instructional activities are given high visibility by the senior administration, their importance is thereby illustrated (Wright and O'Neil, 1994). An evaluative study of the Lilly Endowment Teaching Fellows Program at thirty research universities has illustrated the important impact that supportive senior administrators can have on the way teaching is valued (see Austin, 1992). The results of a recent case study of the efforts of the University of Massachusetts at Amherst to "encourage a culture on campus that values teaching" has also emphasized how important it is for the campus community—especially faculty—to feel that the administration clearly places a high value on teaching (Aitken and Sorcinelli, 1994, p. 64).

Faculty involvement, shared values, and a sense of ownership. The widespread involvement of faculty in every aspect of planning and implementing activities that encourage instructional excellence and improvement is necessary to increase the chances for shared values between administrators and faculty. In-depth case studies of ten liberal arts colleges where faculty were highly committed to teaching revealed that "participatory leadership" and "organizational structures" that encouraged "active involvement of faculty in making important institutional decisions" were common characteristics of the teaching cultures of these exemplary colleges (Rice and Austin, 1990, pp. 28–29). The results of case studies at twelve community colleges have indicated that institutional cultures characterized by shared values between administrators and faculty that are "centered on the importance of promoting student achievement" are the most likely to manifest faculty behaviors that promote student learning (Richardson, 1993, p. 106). Furthermore, among colleges and universities participating in the Bush Foundation Faculty Development Project, institutional cultures characterized by shared faculty-administrative leadership that promoted a sense of "faculty ownership" had the more successful faculty development programs (Eble and McKeachie, 1985, p. 216).

A broader definition of scholarship. After nearly a full century since the construct of scholarship was given its contemporary meaning, recent years have witnessed growing efforts to reconceptualize and expand its meaning (Boyer, 1990; Paulsen and Feldman, 1995b; Schön, 1995). The results of four recent case studies of institutions ranging from a large research university to a small liberal arts college indicate that one of the factors influencing the relationship between the culture of a campus and the value it places on teaching is "an appropriate balance between teaching and scholarship" (Armour, 1995, p. 20). This expanded view "allows faculty to build on their own scholarly strengths and be rewarded for them" (Rice and Austin, 1990, p. 33).

A teaching demonstration or pedagogical colloquium as part of the hiring process. Campus cultures that place a high value on teaching regularly include some demonstration of teaching effectiveness as part of interviewing and hiring new faculty (Jenrette and Napoli, 1994; Rice and Austin, 1988). In a recent survey of faculty development professionals, the policy that "hiring practices require demonstration of teaching ability" was ranked among the top ten institutional practices in terms of its capacity to contribute to the improvement of teaching (Wright and O'Neil, 1994, p. 10).

Frequent interaction, collaboration, and community among faculty. Institutional and departmental cultures that support teaching are characterized by opportunities for frequent interaction among faculty on teaching-related issues. After interviewing eighty-eight faculty members at six research universities, Froh, Menges, and Walker (1993) concluded that one of the important institutional characteristics that can help increase the intrinsic rewards of teaching is the availability of opportunities to talk about teaching. In an eleven-campus study, LaCelle-Peterson and Finkelstein (1993) demonstrated that one of the most important characteristics of a positive teaching culture is the opportunity for collegial interaction and collaboration about teaching. Austin and Baldwin (1991) identified three major benefits for instructors resulting from faculty collaboration in teaching: improvement of teaching ability, increased intellectual stimulation, and reduction in the degree of isolation associated with traditional teaching.

A faculty development program or campus teaching center. Campus cultures that value teaching are characterized by extensive faculty development programs (LaCelle-Peterson and Finkelstein, 1993; Rice and Austin, 1990), often coordinated by the staff of a campus teaching center (Aitken and Sorcinelli, 1994; Ambrose, 1995; Austin, 1990). The resources and programs of teaching centers might include some or all of the following: individual consultations, departmental consultations, workshops, seminars, conferences, teaching assistant training programs, annual award programs, materials on teaching development, and institutional participation in grants and research on teaching and faculty development. In a recent survey, faculty development professionals ranked a campus teaching "center to promote effective instruction" as one of the top ten institutional practices in terms of its capacity to improve teaching (Wright and O'Neil, 1994, p. 10).

Supportive and effective department chairs. One of the most critical characteristics of institutional and departmental cultures that value teaching is the presence of supportive and effective department chairs (Lucas, 1994). Massy, Wilger, and Colbeck (1994) reported a study of faculty across the humanities, social sciences, and science departments that revealed that a supportive department chair is of pivotal importance in creating a culture that values teaching. Similarly, a national sample of faculty development professionals recently ranked the role of the supportive chairperson second out of a possible thirty-six institutional practices (Wright and O'Neil, 1994, p. 15). Rice and Austin (1990) described the essential role of the department chair as follows: "Department chairs can convey to faculty members information about how teaching efforts are valued, how time is most profitably allocated, and on what basis rewards are determined. . . . Without the support of department chairs, many incentives to encourage good teaching may be fruitless" (p. 39).

Connecting rigorous evaluation of teaching to tenure and promotion decisions. Recent case studies have consistently demonstrated that a common and outstanding characteristic of teaching cultures is the rigorous (peer and student) evaluation of teaching and the connection of this evaluation to tenure and promotion decisions (Armour, 1995; Jenrette and Napoli, 1994). Moreover, in a recent international survey of faculty development professionals, respondents identified "recognition of teaching in tenure and promotion decisions" as the top-ranked institutional practice in terms of its "potential to improve the quality of teaching" (Wright and O'Neil, 1995, pp. 12–13). Furthermore, interviews with three hundred faculty on fifteen campuses have revealed that departmental cultures that support teaching quality are more likely to value rigorous peer and student evaluation of teaching and to connect such evaluation to decisions about tenure and promotion (Massy, Wilger, and Colbeck, 1994).

Motivation to Teach Well in the Context of a Supportive Teaching Culture

Studying faculty motivations for teaching is complex, in part because of the many external and internal satisfactions involved, including satisfactions that blend the two kinds of rewards. *External* rewards include granting of tenure, promotion, merit pay, travel provisions, payment of incidental department and professional expenses, clerical assistance, and special privileges (for example, certain kinds of office space or desirable courses or classrooms). These and other external motivators are discussed in Murray (1995) and Knapper (1997). Faculty may also be *intrinsically* motivated to teach. McKeachie (1997) has listed a number of such internal motivators, including liking open-ended problem solving, wanting to be helpful, having a sense of making a difference (such as seeing students develop), feeling satisfaction from interacting with students, feeling a sense of competence (increasing skill and knowledge), having opportunities for learning and to use skills and knowledge, and having autonomy-independence (self-determination).

We will focus briefly on certain intrinsic motivations—namely, faculty members' innate needs for competence and self-determination, their valuing of activities that interest and challenge them, and their seeking of opportunities to learn and achieve (see Austin and Gamson, 1983; Bess, 1977; Deci, Kasser, and Ryan, 1997; Deci and Ryan, 1982; McKeachie, 1997). Particularly important to these motivations is informative feedback from a variety of sources. Our view is that a supportive teaching culture constitutes a context that promotes the availability of informative feedback in various forms about an individual's teaching effectiveness, which in turn stimulates teachers' motivation for instructional excellence.

In a supportive teaching culture, informative feedback is readily available from several sources—colleagues, consultants, chairs, students, and teachers themselves—to address the needs of faculty for self-determination and excellence in teaching, to provide opportunities to learn and achieve, and to stimulate, inform, and support efforts to improve instruction (and to sustain these improvements over time). Exemplary forms of feedback from these various sources have been analyzed more fully in Paulsen and Feldman (1995a).

Colleagues, Consultants, and Chairs as Sources of Informative Feedback. Recent developments in action science, reflective practice, adult learning theory, and the like have encouraged an expanded range of strategies that use colleagues either to help improve teaching or to maintain motivation for instructional excellence (Cranton, 1994). One important set of activities, programs, and projects in this expansion is the renewed use of team teaching (Baldwin and Austin, 1995). Faculty collaboration through team teaching benefits professors by developing or maintaining their teaching abilities, intellectually stimulating them, engaging them as self-directed learners, and more closely connecting them to the university or college as a community. A second set of programs and practices is collegial coaching (Katz and Henry, 1988; Smith and LaCelle-Peterson, 1991). Two primary activities involved in collegial coaching are observation of classroom teaching and instructional consultation (review of course materials as well as discussions about classroom practices) with peers or trained consultants.

Instructional consultation is usually based on a comprehensive model that includes data collection and analysis by the consultant, strategies for improvement that are worked out between the consultant and teacher, and an evaluation phase (Lewis and Povlacs, 1988). Consultation improves teaching and raises motivation to excel in teaching primarily through the use of effective practices in giving feedback (often associated with student ratings and direct observation or videotapes of classroom teaching) and through the various interpersonal roles assumed by consultants (Brinko, 1990, 1991).

Chairs of departments, too, are important to maintaining high motivation and excellent teaching, as well as to improving instruction (when needed). One way they help is by providing support—financial and otherwise—to ongoing formal and informal attempts to improve teaching and to reward existing instructional excellence. Moreover, they are invaluable in defining faculty development and instructional improvement (as distinct from faculty evaluation) as important departmental activities. They may plan programs for the department—such as pedagogical colloquia—that help maintain motivation as well as improve teaching. They can even intervene more directly by following a set of steps similar to those used in instructional consultation (Creswell and others, 1990).

Students as Sources of Informative Feedback. Students are hardly silent partners in affecting motivation of faculty, encouraging superior teaching, or helping improve faculty performance. Research has shown persistently that feedback from student ratings is of value in improving teaching, particularly if this feedback is accompanied by the teacher's consulting with a colleague or a teaching consultant (L'Hommedieu, Menges, and Brinko, 1990). Several different ways of using student interviews for giving feedback to teachers have also been reported as successful. These include group discussion techniques, small-group instructional diagnosis, the class interview, quality-control circles (Tiberius, Sackin, Janzen, and Preece, 1993), and even inviting students into the classroom who are not "official" members of the class but who are trained in classroom observation (Sorenson, 1994). "Classroom assessment" offers a wide range of methods for obtaining useful feedback on what, how much, and how well students are learning (Angelo and Cross, 1993).

How Teachers Can Provide Informative Feedback to Themselves. Because college teachers often have a strong need to seek self-determined competence, their behavior can be understood by viewing them as "reflective practitioners" (Brookfield, 1995; Schön, 1983). Activities that constitute such practice-centered inquiry have been shown to be useful strategies for maintaining motivation to teach well, as well as for improving instruction (Amundsen, Gryspeerdt, and Moxness, 1993). The ultimate foundation of all reflective practice or self-reflection is the ability and opportunity to engage in self-evaluation or self-assessment. Two common methods of collecting self-evaluation feedback at universities involve the use of self-rating forms and self-reports. A second method, self-reports completed by college professors, has traditionally been limited to vitae and reports of activities. The idea of self-reports has been conceptually and functionally expanded into a medium, compendium, and showcase for reflective practice—namely, the teaching dossier or portfolio (which essentially represents an elaborate and reflective form of self-evaluation) (Anderson, 1993; Edgerton, Hutchings, and Quinlan, 1991; Seldin, 1993).

Summary

In this chapter we identified eight characteristics of a campus culture that are supportive of teaching. We then briefly traced how in a supportive teaching culture informative feedback is likely to be readily available to college teachers from different sources—colleagues, consultants, chairs, students, and the teacher himself or herself. Such feedback helps to address the needs of faculty for self-determination and excellence in teaching, to provide opportunities for them to learn and achieve, and to simulate, inform, and support them in efforts to improve their instruction.

References

Aitken, N. D., and Sorcinelli, M. D. "Academic Leaders and Faculty Developers: Creating an Institutional Culture That Values Teaching." *To Improve the Academy,* 1994, *13,* 63–77.

Ambrose, S. A. "Fitting Programs to Institutional Cultures: The Founding and Evolution of the University Teaching Center." In P. Seldin (ed.), *Improving College Teaching.* Bolton, Mass.: Anker, 1995.

Amundsen, C., Gryspeerdt, D., and Moxness, K. "Practice-Centered Inquiry: Developing More Effective Teaching." *Review of Higher Education,* 1993, *16* (3), 329–353.

Anderson, E. (ed.). *Campus Use of the Teaching Portfolio.* Washington, D.C.: American Association for Higher Education, 1993.

Angelo, T. A., and Cross, K. P. *Classroom Assessment Techniques: A Handbook for College Faculty.* San Francisco: Jossey-Bass, 1993.

Armour, R. A. "Using Campus Culture to Foster Improved Teaching." In P. Seldin (ed.), *Improving College Teaching.* Bolton, Mass.: Anker, 1995.

Austin, A. E. *To Leave an Indelible Mark: Encouraging Good Teaching in Research Universities Through Faculty Development.* Nashville, Tenn.: Peabody College of Vanderbilt University, 1990.

Austin, A. E. "Supporting Junior Faculty Through a Teaching Fellows Program." In M. D. Sorcinelli and A. E. Austin (eds.), *Developing New and Junior Faculty.* New Directions for Teaching and Learning, no. 50. San Francisco: Jossey-Bass, 1992.

Austin, A. E., and Baldwin, R. G. *Faculty Collaboration: Enhancing the Quality of Scholarship and Teaching.* ASHE-ERIC Higher Education Report no. 7. Washington, D.C.: School of Education and Human Development, George Washington University, 1991.

Austin, A. E., and Gamson, Z. F. *Academic Workplace: New Demands, Heightened Tensions.* ASHE-ERIC Higher Education Report no. 10. Washington, D.C.: Association for the Study of Higher Education, 1983.

Baldwin, R. G., and Austin, A. E. "Faculty Collaboration in Teaching." In P. Seldin (ed.), *Improving College Teaching.* Bolton, Mass.: Anker, 1995.

Bess, J. L. "The Motivation to Teach." *Journal of Higher Education,* 1977, *48* (3), 243–258.

Boyer, E. L. *Scholarship Reconsidered: Priorities of the Professoriate.* Princeton, N.J.: Carnegie Foundation for the Advancement of Teaching, 1990.

Brinko, K. T. "Instructional Consultation with Feedback in Higher Education." *Journal of Higher Education,* 1990, *61* (1), 65–83.

Brinko, K. T. "The Interactions of Teaching Improvement." In M. Theall and J. Franklin (eds.), *Effective Practices for Improving Teaching.* New Directions for Teaching and Learning, no. 48. San Francisco: Jossey-Bass, 1991.

Brookfield, S. D. *Becoming a Critically Reflective Teacher.* San Francisco: Jossey-Bass, 1995.

Clark, B. R. *The Academic Life: Small Worlds, Different Worlds.* Princeton, N.J.: Carnegie Foundation for the Advancement of Teaching, 1987.

Cranton, P. "Self-Directed and Transformative Instructional Development." *Journal of Higher Education,* 1994, *65* (6), 762–774.

Creswell, J. W., Wheeler, D. W., Seagren, A. T., Egly, N. J., and Beyer, K. D. *The Academic Chairperson's Handbook.* Lincoln: University of Nebraska Press, 1990.

Deci, E. L., Kasser, T., and Ryan, R. M. "Self-Determined Teaching: Opportunities and Obstacles." In J. L. Bess (ed.), *Teaching Well and Liking It: Motivating Faculty to Teach Effectively.* Baltimore: Johns Hopkins University Press, 1997.

Deci, E. L., and Ryan, R. M. "Intrinsic Motivation to Teach: Possibilities and Obstacles in Our Colleges and Universities." In J. L. Bess (ed.), *Motivating Professors to Teach Effectively.* New Directions for Teaching and Learning, no. 10. San Francisco: Jossey-Bass, 1982.

Eble, K. E., and McKeachie, W. J. *Improving Undergraduate Education Through Faculty Development.* San Francisco: Jossey-Bass, 1985.

Edgerton, R., Hutchings, P., and Quinlan, K. *The Teaching Portfolio: Capturing the Scholarship in Teaching.* Washington, D.C.: American Association for Higher Education, 1991.

Froh, R. C., Menges, R. J., and Walker, C. J. "Revitalizing Faculty Work Through Intrinsic Rewards." In R. M. Diamond and B. E. Adam (ed.), *Recognizing Faculty Work: Reward Systems for the Year 2000.* New Directions for Higher Education, no. 81. San Francisco: Jossey-Bass, 1993.

Jenrette, M. S., and Napoli, V. *The Teaching-Learning Enterprise: Miami-Dade Community College's Blueprint for Change.* Bolton, Mass.: Anker, 1994.

Katz, J., and Henry, M. *Turning Professors into Teachers: A New Approach to Faculty Development and Student Learning.* Old Tappan, N.J.: Macmillan, 1988.

Knapper, C. "Rewards for Teaching." In P. Cranton (ed.), *Universal Challenges in Faculty Work: Fresh Perspectives from Around the World.* New Directions for Teaching and Learning, no. 72. San Francisco: Jossey-Bass, 1997.

LaCelle-Peterson, M. W., and Finkelstein, M. J. "Institutions Matter: Campus Teaching Environments' Impact on Senior Faculty." In M. J. Finkelstein and M. W. LaCelle-Peterson (eds.), *Developing Senior Faculty as Teachers.* New Directions for Teaching and Learning, no. 55. San Francisco: Jossey-Bass, 1993.

Lewis, K. G., and Povlacs, J. T. (eds.). *Face to Face: A Sourcebook of Individual Consultation Techniques for Faculty Development Personnel.* Stillwater, Okla.: New Forums Press, 1988.

L'Hommedieu, R., Menges, R. J., and Brinko, K. T. "Methodological Explanations for the Modest Effects of Feedback from Student Ratings." *Journal of Educational Psychology,* 1990, 82 (2), 232–241.

Lucas, A. F. *Strengthening Departmental Leadership: A Team-Building Guide for Chairs in Colleges and Universities.* San Francisco: Jossey-Bass, 1994.

Massy, W. F., Wilger, A. K., and Colbeck, C. "Overcoming 'Hollowed' Collegiality." *Change,* 1994, 26 (4), 11–20.

McKeachie, W. J. "Wanting to Be a Good Teacher: What Have We Learned to Date?" In J. L. Bess (ed.), *Teaching Well and Liking It: Motivating Faculty to Teach Effectively.* Baltimore: Johns Hopkins University Press, 1997.

Murray, J. P. *Successful Faculty Development and Evaluation: The Complete Teaching Portfolio.* ASHE-ERIC Higher Education Report no. 8. Washington, D.C.: Graduate School of Education and Development, George Washington University, 1995.

Paulsen, M. B., and Feldman, K. A. *Taking Teaching Seriously: Meeting the Challenge of Instructional Improvement.* ASHE-ERIC Higher Education Report no. 2. Washington, D.C.: Graduate School of Education and Human Development, George Washington University, 1995a.

Paulsen, M. B., and Feldman, K. A. "Toward a Reconceptualization of Scholarship: A Human Action System with Functional Imperatives." *Journal of Higher Education,* 1995b, 66 (6), 615–640.

Rice, E. R., and Austin, A. E. "High Faculty Morale." *Change,* 1988, 20 (2), 51–58.

Rice, E. R., and Austin, A. E. "Organizational Impacts on Faculty Morale and Motivation to Teach." In P. Seldin and Associates, *How Administrators Can Improve Teaching: Moving from Talk to Action in Higher Education.* San Francisco: Jossey-Bass, 1990.

Richardson, R. C., Jr. "Creating Effective Learning Environments." In M. Weimer (ed.), *Faculty as Teachers.* University Park: National Center on Postsecondary Teaching, Learning, and Assessment, Pennsylvania State University, 1993.

Schön, D. A. *The Reflective Practitioner.* San Francisco: Jossey-Bass, 1983.

Schön, D. A. "The New Scholarship Requires a New Epistemology: Knowing in Action." *Change,* 1995, 27 (6), 26–34.

Schuster, J. H., and Bowen, H. R. "The Faculty at Risk." *Change,* 1985, 17 (5), 13–21.

Seldin, P. *Successful Use of Teaching Portfolios.* Bolton, Mass.: Anker, 1993.

Smith, M. J., and LaCelle-Peterson, M. "The Professor as Active Learner: Lessons from the New Jersey Master Faculty Program." *To Improve the Academy,* 1991, 10, 271–278.

Sorenson, D. L. "Valuing the Student Voice: Student Observer/Consultant Programs." *To Improve the Academy,* 1994, 13, 97–108.

Tiberius, R. G., Sackin, H. D., Janzen, K. R., and Preece, M. "Alliances for Change: A Procedure for Improving Teaching Through Conversations with Learners and Partnerships with Colleagues." *Journal of Staff, Program and Organization Development,* 1993, 11 (1), 11–23.

Wright, W. A., and O'Neil, M. C. "Teaching Improvement Practices: New Perspectives." *To Improve the Academy,* 1994, 13, 5–37.

Wright, W. A., and O'Neil, M. C. "Teaching Improvement Practices: International Perspectives." In W. Wright (ed.), *Teaching Improvement Practices.* Bolton, Mass.: Anker, 1995.

KENNETH A. FELDMAN *is professor of sociology at the State University of New York at Stony Brook.*

MICHAEL B. PAULSEN *is professor of educational leadership at the University of New Orleans.*

This chapter discusses the holistic motivation required to sustain an interdisciplinary learning community at the level required to support a credible and durable program.

Motivation in Interdisciplinary Programs

Edward B. Nuhfer

We easily take for granted the advantages that come with our established disciplines. Disciplines have automatic identity and name recognition either because they have clearly correlative, long-established professions (such as engineering or business) or because they have an established, respected, academic association (such as philosophy or history). A discipline has an established "home" on the campus in a department where students can go for advising, for contact with professors with common interests, and for contact with other students in the same major. Disciplines have at least one established introductory survey course, one that is often a general education requirement. This results in critical masses of students being exposed to the discipline, and some of them will be inspired to study the subject further. Departments also have durability. Even when relationships between personnel in a department are not good, the department is likely to survive.

By contrast, most interdisciplinary programs lack automatic identity, clear space, or curricular territory. Within the curriculum, an interdisciplinary program finds itself in the unenviable position of requiring course contributions from several departments while no unit in the university requires its courses. Faculty who become disenchanted with an interdisciplinary program can usually withdraw support without penalty. Therefore motivation is more closely tied to program success in interdisciplinary programs than in any established discipline.

Why Interdisciplinary Programs Fail

In the record of the environmental education programs of the 1970s and early 1980s (Rajagopal, 1983) we have an excellent source of experience for helping us to understand why interdisciplinary programs fail. In the early 1970s, a plethora of interdisciplinary "environmental" programs were created in varied institutions. Relative to established departments, the life spans of these inter-disciplinary programs were short, and there were clear reasons for their demise.

First, some of these programs failed simply because they should have. Any interdisciplinary program should be established based on no-nonsense ethical principles that include justice (allocating sufficient resources to maintain a sound program), beneficence (serving in students' best interests), fidelity (delivering to students what is promised), nonmalfeasance (doing no harm by using students' time well), and veracity (truthfully defining the relationship of the program to students' aspirations and responsibilities). Although it is wonderful if an interdisciplinary program significantly raises an institution's student enrollments or allows particular faculty members with different interests the opportunity to work together, neither of these benefits justifies founding a program that cannot meet the ethical foundations. Time exposes programs that do not serve students well, and these fail because they should.

Second, interdisciplinary programs fail because of insufficient promotion of their identity. Discipline names such as *chemistry, biology,* or *philosophy* are everyday words from which most people can obtain some meaning that links program with content; but interdisciplinary names such as *reclamation, Headwaters program,* or *population and world resources* are not household words. In 1980, a study by the U.S. Department of Labor and the Environmental Protection Agency revealed that the dismal employment of graduates of interdisciplinary environmental programs resulted largely because employers could not identify the content skills or value of graduates of such programs. So employers hired graduates whose degrees they understood—essentially graduates like themselves from established departments.

Third, interdisciplinary programs fail when the scale, purpose, and capabilities of a program are not continually reviewed. An interdisciplinary program should fill a special niche not well filled by existing programs, and if it is a professional niche, the program should be maintained at the size and quality that maintains optimal reputation through success. A clear niche can provide for excellent career opportunities, but if the program grows greatly beyond the opportunities available, or if it fails to anticipate a change in the niche, then the program reputation may suffer and student enthusiasm and enrollments will plummet.

Fourth, interdisciplinary programs fail because the time and labor involved in motivating constituents to maintain a durable, high-quality program is almost always underestimated. Far more is required to maintain a healthy interdisciplinary program than simply offering the necessary courses.

Motivation as the Key to Avoiding Failure

A principle of motivation noted by Pike (1994) is extremely important: We cannot motivate other people, but we can create environments in which people can motivate themselves. As Wlodkowski notes in Chapter One of this issue, intrinsic motivation is a powerful force. The following common attributes of such intrinsically motivating environments appear in comprehensive discussions of motivation (Maehr and Ames, 1989; Maehr and Kleiber, 1987; Peters and Waterman, 1982).

- Giving positive reinforcement
- Conveying enthusiasm
- Creating awareness of value
- Maintaining global awareness
- Cultivating personal responsibility
- Fostering supportive interpersonal relationships
- Linking individuals' intrinsic self-interest with the program
- Structuring experiences that show real-world relevance

To maintain an interdisciplinary program, motivation must occur at the student level in classes, at the student level outside of class, at the faculty level, at the administrative level, and at the level of the peer professional community off campus.

Motivating Students in Class. Most pedagogical research focuses on motivation inside classrooms (Forsyth and McMillan, 1991), but beyond courses students must be able to value their overall program and understand the unique potential it offers them as a profession or in enrichment of their lives. To achieve this, students need to come together regularly with fellow students with compatible interests. An interdisciplinary program must rely on courses from several areas, but students in an interdisciplinary major frequently find themselves in a minority within their classes. There needs to be a few classes dominated by students of the program itself in order to reinforce the uniqueness of the program and to set it apart from any of the contributing disciplines.

This continuity can be achieved by providing an introductory awareness course followed by an annual "special topics" course in which the themes repeat only every four or more years. A capstone course that really unites the curriculum in some way is extremely beneficial. It could be something as simple as a two-week demonstration field trip or as individual as a senior thesis, but the closure must include unification of disciplines as a capstone.

A good one-credit awareness course might meet in an early evening hour that is not likely to conflict with other classes or require major outlays of time or tuition. Such a course is an excellent place to incorporate the motivational attributes identified earlier. The structure should involve one faculty member (usually the director) as the convener and principal instructor, and a mix of experiences should be provided by additional faculty, students, and the peer professional community. Key faculty should be invited to do presentations about themselves, the courses they offer, and how their disciplines contribute to the interdisciplinary program, and to present examples that illustrate the use of their discipline in an interdisciplinary context. An optional visit to faculty members' labs or departments can be a part of the evening presentation.

Other presenters could include a graduate of the program telling about his or her uses of the learning acquired in the program, a member of the societal peer group informing students of the satisfactions and challenges that await them, and an upperclass student, likely the student club president, talking about how to succeed in the program and identifying available resources for help. A trip off campus where pertinent interdisciplinary knowledge is applied in some way is a great addition to such a course. Each on-campus session should be concluded with a summary by the faculty convener, followed by refreshments and time for informal discussions. Repeated invitations should be given for new students to remain and to join in discussions.

A standing assignment that ties the presentations into the central unifying concept of the program should be planned at the outset. In the one-credit course given at the University of Wisconsin at Platteville for the Reclamation Program (an interdisciplinary four-year major program that spanned three colleges), the final exam question was given out in the first period: "What is reclamation? Illustrate the concepts and applications of reclamation by using information from at least ten of the fourteen presentations you have experienced this term." Students were instructed to maintain a journal that focused on the final exam question and to reflect on it after each session. Students thus built the desired global awareness out of many disciplinary presentations through early disclosure of the learning outcome expected and through a structure that was suited to help build global awareness. The introductory course set the program apart from any one contributing department while providing recognition to all. The ability to query presenters both on the campus and at the localities of peer workers allowed students to obtain personal responses and to make their own informed decisions about personally relevant questions such as "What's in this for me?" and "Does this program meet my needs and my aspirations?"

Motivating Students Outside of Class. "Good practice encourages contacts between students and faculty" is the first of Chickering and Gamson's (1987) well-known *Seven Principles for Good Practice in Undergraduate Education*. In interdisciplinary programs, motivating by forging awareness, enthusiasm, support, and ownership of the educational experience acknowledges the need to provide contact with students outside of class. There are several ways to promote faculty-student contact. For example, motivation in an interdisciplinary program can be effectively inspired through a student academic club. Appreciation of social support and the development of social skills are essential parts of education (Johnson, Johnson, and Smith, 1991). A student club centered around an academic program can convey the attributes of personal responsibility, teamwork, organization, communication, and leadership. A club advisor is provided with the joyous but uncommon opportunity of seeing this growth develop with participating students over several years, and of learning that some attributes can be developed at a deeper level outside of class. Beyond the obvious social support, the club enables motivation to take place on a scale that no individual could accomplish alone. Its weekly meetings can provide the equivalent of a "home" that disciplines enjoy in departments. Through its activities it can convey program identity to the entire campus and wider community. Examples of helpful projects that motivate campus and external constituencies include the following:

- Maintaining a display case or bulletin board with photos and brochures in a well-traveled hallway
- Developing program identification with student-designed T-shirt logos or caps
- Holding joint meetings and projects with student clubs in other departments
- Sponsoring a theme activity such as a natural sciences or humanities banquet that permits the supporting departments to socialize together
- Running thematic interdisciplinary field trips
- Sponsoring fundraisers such as a campuswide dance or cookout hosting a regional academic symposium at the campus
- Sponsoring regional short courses taught by the most reputable campus faculty
- Participating in community activities such as cleanups, blood drives, or adopt-a-highway programs, or in needed campus services such as lab maintenance
- Sponsoring a teacher-of-the-year award and plaque for faculty who contribute excellent courses to their program
- Building a homecoming float
- Recognizing outstanding scholarship or activities of club members by awards such as plaques
- Traveling as a group to a professional meeting and rating speakers in order to select a couple for invitation to speak at the campus
- Building an exhibit and displaying it at a professional meeting
- Identifying a peer professional group, then forming a student chapter of that group, perhaps the first such chapter
- Participating in faculty research as support teams
- Organizing study groups
- Organizing big brother and sister mentors for new students
- Painting a thematic mural in an otherwise ugly stairwell
- Organizing a special session at a state academy of arts, sciences, or letters
- Maintaining internship and job listings and notices
- Authoring a newsletter for distribution to student clubs with similar interests at other campuses, or to the peer professional community
- Recruiting guest speakers for classes and club meetings

The list of meaningful activities that a club can provide to enrich the awareness and experience of students is truly endless.

The director should work with club officers to ensure development of outstanding organizational and leadership skills and to show officers how they can cultivate such skills in younger undergraduates. Students should be encouraged to reach out to professionals off campus, and to have the confidence needed to promote themselves through the unique educational strengths they are acquiring from their program. Initially the director will have to generate the projects and momentum, but as soon as club officers sense the initial benefits, future brainstorming sessions with officers are as likely to have the director following their good ideas as furnishing them.

Motivating Contributing Faculty. Faculty become as motivated as students do by being valued and included. Faculty presentations at the one-credit course permit each faculty member to have exposure to new, incoming students. The exposure is important to students to help them become familiar with supporters of their program, and it is also important to faculty to help them recognize that they will soon be meeting the needs of this particular group of students in their courses. The interdisciplinary program can be a way of unifying entire segments of a campus by sponsoring get-togethers of contributing departments. Faculty who normally have little chance to meet with one another across disciplines will benefit, and a truly satisfying event for them provides recognition of their being valued as contributors to the interdisciplinary program.

The director can invite key faculty to attend a regional or national meeting of the peer professional society, to introduce the faculty to members of that group, and to seek research or collaborative opportunities for those faculty.

Few faculty have been trained to run student academic clubs or manage interdisciplinary programs. Perhaps this accounts for the fact that using time well outside the classroom is an often-neglected aspect of faculty development. If we truly believe that interdisciplinary education is a means of solving interdisciplinary problems, then we must certainly develop faculty who can manage and nurture interdisciplinary programs.

The director can also encourage key faculty to sponsor a special-topics seminar for the interdisciplinary program in a key area. The seminar may involve students in research and allow the faculty member to teach an area of her or his special interest that may not be possible to offer otherwise. When such a seminar is provided, the director should at the very least convey appreciation in writing to the faculty member. A last-day after-class party sponsored by the interdisciplinary program that celebrates the course offering is an excellent way to convey recognition. In colleges where student credit hours are an issue (where isn't this true?), the student credit hours generated by the interdisciplinary program should always be credited back to the department that contributes the faculty. Conflicts of interest stifle enthusiasm and motivation, so it is usually an advantage for an interdisciplinary program never to accumulate student credit hours. Removal of conflicts for credit encourages contribution by supporting departments, which can then take pride in and credit for the success of the interdisciplinary program.

Motivating Administrators. No matter how well departments work together, an interdisciplinary program requires support for resources at the administrative level. Administrators who are not informed about a program cannot be faulted if they are not motivated to help it. For example, grants and foundation office supervisors need to be informed about the nature of the program so they can begin to look for external resources and funding opportunities. The identity crisis inherent in many interdisciplinary programs means that the placement director must be informed about the employment potential of the program's graduates. Do not simply talk to these administrators. Invite them to a club meeting when you have a speaker who epitomizes what the program is about. Take them to dinner with the speaker and a couple of student club officers so they can have a chance truly to absorb both the nature of the program and the excitement of students. Inform top administrators about major accomplishments of the program or of individual students. If a student wins a best-student-paper award, tell your dean and provost in writing. If you host a symposium at your campus, invite your chancellor to provide opening remarks. Try to schedule a presentation with your alumni board, or if regents or trustees review your program, deliver your five-minute report with all the enthusiasm you can muster, and if at all possible, present with a student.

Motivating Societal Peer Groups. Nothing motivates professionals so much as having contact with an enthusiastic group of students. As shown by the 1980 U.S. Department of Labor study, those organizations left to themselves will hire people like themselves. If you can find the professional peer group for your interdisciplinary program, they will be very interested in learning about a program that is training students to think in the same kinds of paradigms they had to discover for themselves. Such peers are invaluable in helping universities to plan interdisciplinary curricula, and the recognition that peers receive by being asked for input is motivation for them to continue their involvement. When peers host a visit at their work site, there is no better way for the program to be remembered than by presenting the peer group members with T-shirts or sweatshirts that bear the logo of the program, and by following that up with a thank-you card signed by all student participants. Peer groups have meetings in which they are delighted to have student help with registration or run audiovisual aids. The result is at least a discounted student registration fee and at best first-name recognition between individual students and some of the profession's best-known people. If you can establish formal recognition by creating a student chapter with your peer group, it is an effort that will repay itself manyfold. If you cannot locate an established peer group but know that there are off-campus peers who share common interests with your program, then establish your own national formal peer group and be among its charter members.

Conclusion: The Roles and Responsibilities of a Director

Directors should have as a goal nothing less than regional recognition for their program. Motivation begins with the basic establishment of an identity, and this mere beginning is no trivial task. Directors must negotiate dedicated space for students, the most critical of which is a student lounge and an exhibit case in a well-traveled hallway. A wise director will share ownership by assembling a steering committee composed of key faculty and by creating the student club that serves as a focal point for academic cohesiveness, social support, and recreation. Interdisciplinary directors should not take on the task of placing students in jobs. Instead, directors should work with university placement directors to take advantage of institutional programs and to encourage self-placement through student clubs and professional peer groups.

Unlike deans or chairpersons, interdisciplinary directors have few resources and little control over the people on whom they depend. Consequently they must advance their program entirely through motivation, utilizing enthusiasm, management skill, and superb communication to cultivate good relationships and build consensus. If they can build programs that achieve regional or national recognition, this reputation provides leverage for long-term support. Interdisciplinary programs rely on cooperation, so directors must remain apart from conflicts between departments or deans. Motivation of students requires enthusiastic faculty. If some faculty needed for the program come from departments that are not good at nurturing enthusiasm, then the director needs to nurture it. Furthering identity of the program off-campus provides limitless opportunities to involve students in fascinating activities that promote their interests.

In short, motivation in interdisciplinary programs is established by growing a learning community that involves students, faculty, administrators, and the societal peer group. When successful, the motivation results in a shared vision that is sufficient to ensure the long-term vitality of the program.

References

Chickering, A. W., and Gamson, Z. F. *Seven Principles for Good Practice in Undergraduate Education.* Racine, Wis.: Wingspread Group, Johnson Foundation, 1987.

Forsyth, D. R., and McMillan, J. H. "Practical Proposals for Motivating Students." In R. J. Menges and M. D. Svinicki, (eds.), *College Teaching: From Theory to Practice.* New Directions for Teaching and Learning, no. 45. San Francisco: Jossey-Bass, 1991.

Johnson, D. W., Johnson, R. T., and Smith, K. A. *Active Learning: Cooperation in the College Classroom.* Edina, Minn.: Interaction, 1991.

Maehr, M., and Ames, C. (eds.). *Advances in Motivation and Achievement.* Greenwich, Conn.: JAI Press, 1989.

Maehr, M., and Kleiber, D. A. (eds.). *Advances in Motivation and Achievement.* Vol. 5: *Enhancing Motivation.* Greenwich, Conn.: JAI Press, 1987.

Peters, T. J., and Waterman, R. H., Jr. *In Search of Excellence: Lessons from America's Best-Run Companies.* New York: Warner Books, 1982.

Pike, R. W. *Creative Training Techniques Handbook.* (2nd ed.) Minneapolis, Minn.: Lakewood Books, 1994.

Rajagopal, R. "Environmental Education in the Marketplace: A Decade of U.S. Experience." *Environmental Conservation,* 1983, *10,* 225–230.

U. S. Department of Labor and U. S. Environmental Protection Agency. *Environmental Protection Careers Guidebook: Employment and Training Administration.* Washington, D.C.: U. S. Department of Labor, 1980.

EDWARD B. NUHFER is director of the Office of Teaching Effectiveness and Faculty Development at the University of Colorado at Denver and a professor of geology.

The case study reported in this chapter is an example of both implementing and sustaining change. What motivated faculty at King's College to engage in activities leading to institutional improvement rather than simply engaging in rhetoric?

Institutional Improvement and Motivated Faculty: A Case Study

Donald W. Farmer

King's College is engaged in realizing a paradigm shift from a teaching-centered to a learning-centered campus culture. This transition clarifies institutional mission by understanding that institutional purpose relates more to producing student learning than to providing instruction. King's College has been able to articulate and implement a vision that has the potential not only to provide a unique experience for students but also to be a beacon for other colleges and universities seeking to improve both the quality and quantity of student learning.

Motivating faculty to contribute to institutional improvement does not take place in a vacuum. The campus culture and the climate for change provide the essential conditions in which motivation takes place. When King's College began this transition from a teaching-centered to a learning-centered culture, it was tapping into an existing campus culture of student-centeredness in order to raise faculty consciousness of the logical next steps to improve student learning. Change was not motivated by financial, enrollment, or external pressures.

The Project for Institutional Improvement

The major activity serving as a catalyst for the paradigm shift at King's College was the development in the early 1980s of an outcomes-oriented general education curriculum, supported by course-embedded assessment and student-centered teaching strategies. The previous curriculum, based on distribution requirements, had over the years become a smorgasbord of learning, with a diminished sense of coherence and integrity. A description of the principal

NEW DIRECTIONS FOR TEACHING AND LEARNING, no. 78, Summer 1999 © Jossey-Bass Publishers actions taken to realize this paradigm shift will serve as the case study for exploring strategies and conditions responsible for motivating King's College faculty both to implement and to sustain change. This initiative is described more fully in *Enhancing Student Learning* (Farmer, 1988).

Renewing the curriculum has long been recognized as an effective means of capturing faculty interest and harnessing faculty energies in the service of institutional improvement. The specific design principles used at King's College included the following:

- Understand curriculum as a plan of learning, not merely a collection of courses.
- Provide sequential and cumulative learning.
- Encourage transferable learning across the curriculum.
- Design the curriculum as a matrix by integrating skill development into subject matter courses.
- Implement student-centered teaching strategies to foster active rather than passive learning.
- Develop qualitative, performance-based course-embedded assessment strategies both to assess student learning and to increase student learning.
- Define mastery learning as the ability to apply prior learning to a new stimulus.

These design principles required developing all new courses. To begin this work, project teams composed of faculty from more than one discipline were created. Only after reaching consensus regarding desired learning outcomes did the project teams turn to identifying appropriate course content. Faculty also recognized that for students to meet the challenge provided by an outcomes-oriented curriculum, student-centered teaching strategies needed to be implemented to help students advance from being passive learners to being active learners.

Just as the curriculum design was intended to provide a plan of learning, so also was the assessment model. The King's College course-embedded assessment model makes assessment an integral part of the teaching and learning process. Qualitative assessment is a natural response to teaching and learning—one in which a good assessment strategy is also a good teaching strategy (Farmer, 1993a). Being both diagnostic and supportive of student learning, the qualitative assessment strategies reveal students' strengths and weaknesses as well as empowering students to act on systematic feedback to achieve academic success. The components of the assessment model include the following:

- Pre- and post-assessments for all general education courses
- Four-year competence growth plans designed to integrate the transferable skills of liberal learning (writing, critical thinking, information literacy, and so on) into subject matter courses both in general education and the major program
- A sophomore-junior diagnostic project embedded in a required course in each major
- A more sophisticated senior-level integrated assessment experience embedded in a seminar or capstone course

Assessment contributes to improving student learning by encouraging faculty to make explicit learning goals and criteria for judging student performance. Assessment criteria serve to clarify for students the qualitative level of faculty expectations.

Developing Trust and Sustaining Change

Change is threatening for most people and therefore creates anxiety and invites resistance. Although many factors contribute to the development of a positive organizational climate for change, a condition of trust must be present if efforts to motivate faculty are to succeed. Trust is a prerequisite for creating a positive attitude toward change on a college campus. Building trust is a slow process, requiring the mutual respect of faculty and administrators. Why is creating trust so important? The answer lies in the fact that motivating faculty to contribute to institutional improvement, and ideally to take charge of change, requires risk taking. A condition of trust is a necessary prerequisite to empowering faculty to engage in risk (Farmer, 1990).

Acceptance of the idea of creativity of error—learning derived from an experiment that fails—captures operationally one measure for determining the existence of a condition of trust. It requires an acceptance that valuable lessons can be learned from unsuccessful as well as successful experiments. Faculty must know that their efforts at experimenting and risk taking will be acknowledged and rewarded without penalty if specific initiatives fail.

Unfortunately, many worthwhile innovations in higher education are short-lived or lose their vitality over time. One explanation for this phenomenon is that the level of attention given to implementing change is not continued to meet the challenge of sustaining change. Although many faculty are motivated to participate in implementing new ideas or projects, most initiatives cannot be sustained by goodwill. Colleges need to ensure that the reward system affirms the behaviors needed both to implement and to sustain change. They need to reward pedagogical and curricular experiments of faculty, not just traditional scholarship and publications. Contradictory reward systems sap the psychic energy of faculty that is so vital to maintaining support for innovations.

The ability to sustain change at King's College is due primarily to designing a faculty reward system that mixes intrinsic and extrinsic incentives. Curricular reform and pedagogical experimentation, long recognized as stimuli for tapping the intrinsic motivational energies of a teaching faculty, have been wedded to significant changes in personnel policies—the time-honored source of extrinsic incentives for faculty performance (Farmer, 1993b). Performance appraisal and compensation policies, such as merit pay and senior faculty review culminating in individually funded professional growth plans, reflect intrinsic faculty motivation. Whereas many faculty at King's are opposed philosophically to participating in the merit pay program, the same faculty willingly participate in the senior faculty review process, revealing a strong sense of pride in having been active participants in the transformation of King's College from a teaching-centered to a learning-centered campus culture.

Faculty members supporting institutional improvement became the chief beneficiaries of external funding awarded to the college, receiving courseload reductions, summer stipends for further work in curriculum development, and financial support to attend a variety of national conferences and workshops. These extrinsic rewards complemented intrinsic rewards experienced by faculty, from the positive response of audience and reader respectively when making presentations at professional meetings to publishing articles on the role of King's College faculty as change agents.

Leadership for Change

The institutional environment is also directly shaped by the quality of institutional leadership. Motivating faculty to participate in significant institutional improvement requires that they have confidence in their institutional leaders, especially the principal change agent. Without such confidence, faculty will be reluctant to invest the time and energy required.

Planned change will not take place without the presence of an effective change agent. The effective change agent is one who understands the organization—its values, its resources, and its politics. As a principal campus leader, the change agent must generate confidence and earn the trust of those to be affected by an intended change. The credibility of the change agent is a crucial factor in creating a favorable climate in which to successfully motivate faculty. A change agent must have a good sense of timing, waiting for the opportune moment rather than acting spontaneously. It is equally important to keep the lines of communication open in order to make informed decisions. The change agent must also share credit for successful changes with faculty in order to create enthusiasm and a wider sense of ownership for change among faculty.

Campus leaders need to understand that rhetoric cannot be a substitute for action and that leadership is action and not position. The effective change agent must also serve as a role model for change. Being directly involved with faculty in developing and implementing activities helps to establish the change agent's credibility and the importance of the intended change. A prerequisite for motivating faculty to take action is to convince them that a common purpose for institutional improvement exists for both faculty and the change agent. When confidence and respect have been earned, the change agent can encourage and coach others to transform a vision into a palpable reality.

Strategies for Motivating Faculty

Much of the literature on change indicates that to implement successfully a paradigm shift of the magnitude described in this case study—motivating faculty to transform a campus culture from being teaching centered to being learning centered—requires not only vision but also a crisis. The stimulus for the vision was presented to me as a change agent in the late 1960s when a graduating senior gave the following unsolicited advice: "There is a lot more teaching going on around here than learning and you ought to do something about that!" There was no sense of crisis for faculty because the college enjoyed a strong enrollment and a healthy financial position. Yet the problem stated by the student unmasked a hidden crisis for a faculty proudly proclaiming itself to be a teaching faculty.

Raising Faculty Awareness of the Need for Change. The challenge for the change agent in this context was to raise faculty awareness of the need for change by increasing their level of discomfort with the status quo. The change agent's goal was to tap the intrinsic motivational energy of faculty to provide students with the best possible education. The first step was to ask faculty to review the existing curriculum for general education to discover its strengths and weaknesses. The critique that emerged from that review focused on students' perceptions of the curriculum as a disjointed collection of courses without specific liberal learning objectives, of the absence of a common educational experience, and of the lack of a recommended sequence of courses. Faculty concluded that students would be better served by a reconceptualization of the curriculum rather than by faculty engaging in a traditional political approach to curriculum revision.

A second action was for the change agent to prepare a position paper to launch a campuswide discussion on the question, "What does it mean to be a teaching faculty?" This question sparked provocative faculty reflection and discussion on the role of faculty as disseminators of information versus facilitators of student learning. The resulting dialogue helped faculty to recognize the impending paradigm shift in higher education. Moreover, this initiative helped faculty to understand that to improve student learning required going beyond curriculum reform to an examination of specific pedagogical strategies appropriate to fostering desired student learning outcomes. A subsequent series of position papers focused faculty attention on student learning outcomes by posing the question, "What will it mean in the twenty-first century to be educated?" Both of these questions were chosen because they built on the most salient components of campus culture and forced faculty to experience a higher level of discomfort with the status quo. This motivated faculty to go beyond the traditional rhetoric associated with the reform of liberal learning in order to engage in concrete actions leading to improvement of both the quality and quantity of student learning.

Preparing Faculty Through Campus-Based Faculty Development. Many worthwhile changes in higher education have failed because changes have been introduced prematurely. The learning style of most faculty members requires information and a rationale in order to understand and accept a proposed change. Time for investigation, questions, dialogue, and reflection is essential. It is equally important that faculty be prepared to implement a proposed change. A change agent should never ask faculty to implement a change unless they are prepared professionally to do so successfully. Faculty need to feel self-confident in order to implement change. Above all, faculty want to avoid the risk of professional embarrassment in the classroom.

Directed and focused faculty development has been a significant ingredient at King's College to prepare faculty to implement change successfully as well as to motivate faculty to take action. The words *directed* and *focused* are important for identifying clear objectives for campus-based faculty development programs. Training in computer literacy, critical thinking, information literacy, and writing across the curriculum are examples of the kind of training required of faculty who need increasingly to take responsibility for the total education of students. King's faculty also participated in a series of workshops over an eight-year period to explore student-centered teaching strategies. Of equal importance in motivating faculty was the development of individual professional growth plans for faculty. These plans were developed by faculty to further the scholarship of teaching and to relate their individual professional goals to institutional objectives such as experimenting with student-centered teaching strategies.

Minimizing Risk for Faculty. Risk is inherent in every successful change. Many faculty, however, have a need to feel in charge of change. Incremental change through pilot testing proved to be a powerful strategy. It allowed time for faculty to gather additional information and to evaluate the feasibility of an intended change before having to make a stronger commitment to the proposed change. Pilot testing lowers risk and therefore helps to motivate faculty to be open to and to participate in changes leading to institutional improvement.

Another strategy utilized at King's College for minimizing risk for faculty was to provide psychological support for innovators. This was achieved by developing faculty project teams for each discrete activity contributing to the paradigm shift from a teaching-centered to a learning-centered campus culture. A project team is distinct from a committee. It is composed of individuals who feel empowered because they set their own agenda to implement change rather than writing a report recommending actions for others to take. A project team is an excellent support group for faculty innovators.

Enlisting Faculty Leaders. Gaining support of a critical mass of faculty is necessary for implementing meaningful change on a college campus. The concept of critical mass is different, however, from that of a simple majority. The critical mass is composed of faculty opinion makers who have the ability to attract the support or who enjoy the tolerance of other faculty. Support from faculty opinion makers motivates other faculty to give the change agent a window of tolerance that provides the necessary time in which to experiment. Involving faculty leaders in pilot tests motivates other faculty to become involved as well.

The fine art of persuasion is certainly a powerful tool of the change agent in winning support for change and in overcoming inertia. The change agent must also have the ability, however, to develop a self-renewal capacity among those involved in order to sustain the change. The credibility of the change agent with faculty is one of the crucial factors in determining the level of this support.

Leveraging External Opportunities. Professional and institutional pride serve as powerful sources of motivation for faculty. Opportunities to tap into these sources of motivation are provided by external opportunities such as accreditation visits, developing grant proposals, and making presentations at meetings of professional organizations. Each of these external opportunities provides an opportunity to showcase a proposed change or a change in progress and to increase the sense of ownership by participating faculty. A favorable judgment by all of these external organizations—praise from a visiting team representing an accrediting agency, the awarding of funding by a foundation, or the acceptance of a proposal for presentation at a professional meeting—can be leveraged on the college campus to increase faculty motivation to support change contributing to institutional improvement.

This strategy was put to good use at King's College. Two visiting teams representing the Middle States Association praised efforts to implement an outcomes-oriented curriculum and a course-embedded assessment program as well as student-centered teaching strategies to help students become active learners. Major funding for these activities followed from successful grant proposals presented to federal agencies and private foundations. The requirement for dissemination by one of the private foundations led to the development of successful presentations at meetings of professional organizations as well as to the preparation of journal articles by faculty. These positive external judgments were widely publicized on campus and served not only as a source of pride for faculty but also as intrinsic sources of motivation for faculty to sustain their commitment to the larger paradigm shift from a teaching-centered to a learning-centered campus culture.

Faculty Perspectives on Motivation for Institutional Improvement

An open-ended survey was administered to a cross-section of senior faculty asking them to respond to the question, "What motivates faculty at King's College to engage in activities leading to institutional improvement rather than simply engaging in rhetoric?" There was a 45 percent response rate to this survey. The timing of the survey was such that the responses were received after the preceding portion of this chapter was written. This permitted keeping the views of the author separate from those of the faculty. Although distinct, both perspectives reveal substantial agreement. The responses suggest six major factors contributing to faculty motivation: a campus culture emphasizing effective teaching and student centeredness, high expectations of faculty colleagues for continuous improvement, a sense of faculty being in control of the implementation of change, support of academic administrators for faculty to experiment, faculty confidence in the change agent, and intrinsic rewards experienced by faculty as a result of positive feedback from external sources.

The following comments from the survey have been selected to provide definition to these reasons that motivate faculty to engage in change. The actual voices of King's faculty also communicate the degree of self-confidence and the level of enthusiasm so important to implementing change successfully.

Campus culture. "I think that first and foremost is my concern for students. When I became a teacher, I knew I wanted to help students learn; I soon realized that what helped them to learn were their opportunities to perform rather than my performance as a dispenser of information. I believe that even more now. Because I have witnessed significant student learning as a result of their performances, I am eager to find additional strategies."

High expectations of faculty colleagues. "I am motivated to improve the quality of my teaching because colleagues whom I admire demand it of me. I am challenged to keep up with them. We talk about teaching even in the most casual settings. I am always picking up new ideas. I find myself eager to share something that really worked for my students. We share stories."

Need of faculty to have a sense of control. "Positive outcomes of an action are not motivating unless a faculty member feels an internal sense of control. Administrative initiatives in the areas of curriculum, assessment, and pedagogy at King's have always passed control and authority to the faculty; edicts have not been issued; the whole process has been in the context of partnership. The faculty sense of ownership of the process of change has been fostered by the high visibility given to faculty colleagues as they travel to other institutions and national conferences to explain our experiments in curriculum, teaching, and assessment."

Academic leadership. "Good leadership has produced good results. What I find motivating is the atmosphere of experimentation that permeates King's College. It is very enabling to work in an environment that encourages the faculty to try new things and to have it be recognized and supported that not all of these experiments will work. Those who propose change seem to genuinely believe in what they are doing. New ideas are presented rationally and convincingly. I have seen in other colleges a tendency for 'idea' people to overburden their staffs with responsibility for carrying out someone else's ideas. Here, academic officials pull their own weight by doing much of the preliminary work, making it easier for faculty to translate new ideas into actions."

Faculty confidence in the change agent. "Because [the change agent's] track record is so good, I trust him when he proposes further change. I believe [the change agent's] dedication, foresight, hard work, and willingness to compensate faculty in a variety of ways has motivated faculty to engage in change. Not only does [the change agent] model innovation at King's through his own teaching and assessment practices, he also creates conditions which facilitate the ongoing development of faculty. Many faculty members are motivated to become change agents because they are asked to do so by someone they respect."

Intrinsic rewards. "It is especially motivating and rewarding to be asked to present my work to faculty colleagues from other institutions. It has always been somewhat surprising but also very gratifying that King's presentations are so positively received by others. Talk about a motivator! I feel rewarded as a member of the faculty when I see the attention that King's receives in national magazines. And I feel rewarded by the positive and flattering comments made in the 1994 regional accreditation report by the visiting team representing the Middle States Association."

Transferable Insights from the King's College Experience

The case study reported in this chapter is an example of both implementing and sustaining change successfully. What are the lessons to be learned from this experience?

Climate for change. One of the clearest lessons to be learned from the King's College case study is the importance of creating a favorable campus climate for change as a prerequisite for utilizing specific change strategies successfully. The existence of trust both permits and motivates faculty to engage in risk taking.

Faculty ownership of change. Systemic change does not happen accidentally. One needs to plan and to strategize. Successful change cannot be imposed on faculty from outside, however. The most powerful motivation to engage in change, especially strategies for implementing academic change, arises within faculty when they feel they are in control of change.

Intrinsic and extrinsic rewards. Striking a balance between intrinsic and extrinsic rewards recognizes that faculty are motivated by a range of complex factors. The power of intrinsic reward to motivate faculty needs to be better understood.

Role of change agent. Academic leadership is critical to implementing and sustaining change. The effective change agent needs to command the respect and confidence of the faculty in order to serve in the multiple roles of catalyst, facilitator, resource linker, and confidence builder. When successful, the change agent develops faculty change agents to take responsibility for implementing change and to reduce the prominence of the principal change agent.

References

Farmer, D. W. *Enhancing Student Learning: Emphasizing Essential Competencies in Academic Programs.* Wilkes-Barre, Pa.: King's College Press, 1988.

Farmer, D. W. "Strategies for Change." In D. W. Steeples (ed.), *Managing Change in Higher Education.* New Directions for Higher Education, no. 71. San Francisco: Jossey-Bass, 1990.

Farmer, D. W. "Course-Embedded Assessment: A Teaching Strategy to Improve Student Learning." *Assessment Update,* 1993a, 5 (1), 8, 10–11.

Farmer, D. W. "Designing a Reward System to Promote the Career Development of Senior Faculty." In M. J. Finkelstein and M. W. LaCelle-Peterson (ed.), *Developing Senior Faculty as Teachers.* New Directions for Teaching and Learning, no. 55. San Francisco: Jossey-Bass, 1993b.

DONALD W. FARMER *is vice president for academic affairs at King's College, Wilkes-Barre, Pennsylvania.*

PART FOUR

Conclusions

Motivational models dealing with teaching, learning, instructional process, and institutional change are very similar. Even when different terms are used, the underlying concepts are the same. What can we learn from these various models?

What Have We Learned? A Synthesis and Some Guidelines for Effective Motivation in Higher Education

Michael Theall, Jennifer Franklin

This volume of *New Directions for Teaching and Learning* begins with Raymond Wlodkowski's overview of motivational issues. Wlodkowski proposes a model with four components: establishing inclusion, developing attitude, enhancing meaning, and engendering competence. He emphasizes a balance between individualistic and socio-constructive approaches to motivation, noting that an understanding of both approaches allows for more effective teaching and learning. Wlodkowski also emphasizes the importance of intrinsic motivation, stating, "In learning, intrinsic motivation occurs when the activity and milieu of learning elicit motivation in the student." It follows from this approach that teachers, administrators, and those who seek to support and enhance the performance of others would find greatest success through a combination of awareness of the individual differences and backgrounds of those with whom they work, and the creative organization of situations and stimuli that have the greatest potential to elicit both the productive motivational responses and the subsequent effort that increase the likelihood of success. As readers of this volume will discover, the positive benefits of effective motivational practice do not stop with increased interest or effort. There is a synergistic cycle of factors that promotes shared ownership and responsibility, expectancy for success, persistence, achievement, and satisfaction.

In this chapter we review and summarize the motivational models, issues, and strategies suggested by other contributors in order to demonstrate their interrelationships and show how, even though the terms used are sometimes different, all the models proposed here have strongly similar conceptual themes. We also consider the common themes and models from this volume with respect to other important contemporary work by researchers in higher education and motivation.

A Matrix of Motivational Constructs

To simplify the task of discussing more than a dozen perspectives that relate to motivation, we have extracted some key principles from each and expressed these as one-word descriptors. These terms are arrayed in Table 10.1 in an author-by-factor matrix. The first nine authors listed are the contributors to this volume; they are listed in the order in which their chapters appear. The names of individual or first authors are used to save space. See the table's footnotes for complete information about authorship.

The terms on the left side of the matrix were developed in one of three ways: they were taken directly from the sources (for example, from the chapters by Wlodkowski, Keller, MacKinnon, and Farmer), they were reduced from longer lists (for example, from the chapters by Panitz, Feldman and Paulsen, and Nuhfer, and from Theall and others, Forsyth and McMillan, and Chickering and Gamson), or they were used to refer to other terms, variables, or factors considered in research reported by the authors (for example, in the chapters by Paulsen and Feldman, and Donald). The terms are grouped on the basis of their face-value relationship to each other, and on the left side of the matrix italics are used to identify categorical titles. The first four category titles are the terms from Wlodkowski's lead chapter because that chapter provides the overview discussion of motivation for this volume. The terms *leadership* and *satisfaction* are taken directly from other authors in the volume.

Because some of the matrix terms are taken directly from the chapters of this volume, little discussion is necessary. The authors explain their models in their respective chapters and these explanations need not be repeated here. The other matrix terms came from authors who have offered somewhat more detailed lists. We will leave readers to explore the extended lists in the chapters by Panitz, Feldman and Paulsen, and Nuhfer, but we will explain how the work of the remaining authors relates to the matrix.

Syntheses. Theall, Birdsall, and Franklin (1997) reviewed motivational models and research and propose five basic elements in effective motivation of learning: designing instruction with students' needs and interests in mind, exciting students' interest and curiosity, clearly organizing and structuring course material, being interested in and supportive of student learning, and providing students with feedback. Included under these general headings are items concerned with inclusion, interest, relevance, value, expectancy, high expectations of students, structure, feedback, and support. All of these terms either duplicate or closely match other terms in the matrix drawn from other sources cited in this volume.

Table 10.1. Motivation Terms: Author by Factor Matrix

Author / Factor	Wlodkowski	Paulsen[a]	Donald	Keller	MacKinnon	Panitz	Feldman[b]	Nuhfer	Farmer	Theall[c]	Pintrich	Forsyth[d]	Chickering[e]
Inclusion	X												
Community			X		X	X	X			X		X	X
Climate		X			X		X		X				X
Ownership								X	X				X
Attitude	X												
Affect		X	X			X					X		
Interest										X			
Awareness			X	X				X					
Attention								X					
Enthusiasm													X
Meaning	X												
Relevance		X	X	X	X					X	X		X
Value										X	X	X	X
Competence	X												
Empowerment		X			X	X						X	
Confidence		X		X								X	
Expectancy			X							X	X		
Leadership									X				
High expectations			X			X	X			X		X	X
Structure							X	X		X			X
Feedback							X	X		X			X
Support												X	
Satisfaction						X							
Rewards				X					X			X	

[a] Paulsen and Feldman (Chapter Two).
[b] Feldman and Paulsen (Chapter Seven).
[c] Theall, Birdsall, and Franklin, 1997.
[d] Forsyth and McMillan, 1991.
[e] Chickering and Gamson, 1987.

Forsyth and McMillan (1991), in an earlier issue of this journal, offered "Practical Proposals for Motivating Students." Their model contained the following items: stress on intrinsic motivation, creating mastery and minimizing fear of failure, encouraging attributions to controllable causes, helping students to set realistic goals, and increasing the value of academic goals. Each of these items fits within the framework of the matrix and thus adds to the consistency of the motivational approaches it suggests.

Chickering and Gamson's (1987) "Seven Principles for Good Practice in Undergraduate Education" are some of the best known and frequently cited general guidelines for higher education. Their principles include emphasis on faculty-student contact, cooperation among students, and respect for diverse talents and ways of learning, which relate to community and inclusion in the matrix; encouraging active learning, which relates to ownership, interest, and relevance in the matrix; emphasis on time on task and high expectations, which relate to structure and high expectations in the matrix; and providing prompt feedback, which relates to the feedback item in the matrix. The Chickering and Gamson model provides further evidence that there is motivational consistency in a wide array of models for higher education.

Motivationally Related Research. Some of the matrix terms were derived from the original research reported by Paulsen and Feldman and by Donald in this volume, and by Pintrich (1989 and in earlier reports). In Chapter Two, Paulsen and Feldman consider student epistemological beliefs and how these beliefs relate to motivation. Among their variables they include intrinsic and extrinsic goal orientation, task value, control of learning, self-efficacy, and test anxiety. They list as productive epistemological beliefs the notions that knowledge is complex and gradually acquired, and that ability can be enhanced. In their presentation of analysis of the correlations of beliefs to motivational constructs, the most powerful findings show intrinsic goal orientation, task value, control of learning, and self-efficacy to be related to the development of productive epistemological beliefs. The terms they use are related to matrix terms as follows: control of learning with ownership, relevance, and empowerment; efficacy with confidence and competence; and task value with value. Thus even though their approach is different, Paulsen and Feldman's findings mesh with the conceptualizations of the motivational factors identified by the other contributors.

Particularly in the area of the control of learning, one is reminded of the work of Weiner (for example, 1986) and Perry (for example, 1991). The causal attributions that students make in the face of success or failure have been shown to differ with respect to the locus (internal or external), stability (stable or unstable), and controllability (controllable or uncontrollable) of those attributions. Students with a record of academic difficulty may develop patterns of attributions that are self-defeating—that is, attributions to external, unstable, and uncontrollable causes. In severe cases, students exhibit "learned helplessness" (for example, Dweck, 1975). Perry (1991) reports that "attributional retraining" is possible wherein students are trained to accept the responsibility for their progress and to realize the direct connection between their effort and their success. Retraining was shown to be especially helpful for these students, allowing them to avoid harmful attributional patterns and to adopt more motivationally productive approaches. The newly productive attributions of such students parallel the foci of the epistemological beliefs that Paulsen and Feldman discuss.

In Chapter Three, Janet Donald reports on an investigation into motivation for higher-order learning. She notes four student orientations toward learning that have been drawn from international research. The first is toward deep or meaningful learning; the second is toward surface learning, emphasizing the reproduction of information; the third is an achievement orientation, concerned with competition and grades; and the last is a nonacademic orientation that includes negative attitudes about learning and disorganized study habits. Because the meaning orientation is the most productive vis-à-vis higher-order learning, it is included with meaning as framed by Wlodkowski in Chapter One. Meaning, in Donald's definition, is also related to expectancy, another term in the matrix.

In her description of factors affecting higher-order learning, Donald includes course goals and student awareness of goals. The former is a direct part of the structure and organization of curricula and courses and thus fits well with the term *structure*, while the latter fits well with the attitudinal awareness component.

Finally, Donald notes differences arising from the disciplines of the students: in this case, physics and engineering. Donald says, "Context and student preparation have a greater effect on achievement than does motivation" (as measured by students' approaches to studying). This observation is consistent with that of Smart and Feldman (1998), who considered the accentuation effects of dissimilar academic departments in an exploration of Holland's (1985) theory. Holland proposed four academic "sub-environments": investigative, artistic, social, and enterprising; and Smart and Feldman, using the notion that these sub-environments accentuated existing predispositions, interests, or orientations, concluded that their results "provide strong support for the validity of Holland's . . . premise that students search for and select academic sub-environments that are compatible with their distinctive patterns of abilities and interests" (1998, p. 410). The motivational implication of the studies is that context can either reduce or enhance the opportunities for student comfort, acculturation, perseverance, inclusion, and success. Clearly there is a relationship of these factors to motivation, and with respect to the matrix these studies add to the weight of the term *community*.

Pintrich and others (1988) developed the Motivated Strategies for Learning Questionnaire (MSLQ). The instrument measures motivational constructs in three general areas: value (including intrinsic and extrinsic goal orientation and task value), expectancy (including control, competence, self-efficacy, and expectancy for success), and affect (dealing with test anxiety). Pintrich (1989) paraphrases with the questions, "Why am I doing this task?" "Can I do this task?" and "How do I feel about this task?" Once again, there is a close relationship between these terms and those proposed by other writers in this volume and elsewhere, and because the MSLQ has been widely used in motivational research, its components add to the consistency of the matrix.[1]

Related Research from Other Perspectives. There are many intriguing avenues of research that are not directly motivational but that support the motivational picture developed in this volume. These include investigations into disciplinary differences, the evaluation of teaching, the value of academic work, and attributional research. A sampling follows.

Gillmore (1994) proposes an approach involving a ratio of time spent preparing for class to how much of that time was considered valuable by students. The "time valued" ratio was significantly correlated (r approaching .50) with student ratings of instruction. Using Gillmore's construct as a base and adding disciplinary differences as a variable, Franklin and Theall (1995) reported regression analyses showing not only that time valued was a powerful predictor of overall ratings, but also that its power varied across disciplines. In other investigations of disciplinary differences, instructional methods, and ratings, Cashin (1990) reported a consistent historic pattern of disciplinary rankings based on average ratings of courses and teachers. Franklin and Theall (1992) further explored these differences and included instructional objectives, methods, and assessment choices among the variables. Consistent patterns were found wherein those disciplines at the high end of the ratings scale used objectives at the analysis-synthesis-evaluation end of Bloom and others' (1956) taxonomy, employed active learning and related methods, and used assessments concentrating on complex tasks, projects, and extended written work. Disciplines at the low end of the ratings scale more frequently used lower order objectives (knowledge-principles-applications), employed lecturing as the predominant instructional method, and relied on midterm and final exams to assess student progress.

The implications of this work relate directly to the notions of *community, value, climate, relevance,* and *structure* in the matrix and also to issues surrounding *attitude, confidence, expectancy, feedback,* and *satisfaction.* For example, in those disciplines that use lecture and midterm and final exams, mechanisms for faculty contact and feedback may be reduced (often as a result of the related issue of class size). Students' confidence in their abilities or in their expectations for success may also suffer. The relevance and meaning and value of the content may not be as apparent because of limited opportunities to become aware of or to truly understand course goals. Student involvement in and ownership of the responsibility for learning are reduced even though the situation seems to be one in which this responsibility is left to students. The difference, of course, is that simply leaving students to "sink or swim" does little to support their acceptance of responsibility or the development of the expectation that their efforts will result in success. Under these conditions, it is not inappropriate to assume lower levels of performance, reduced expectancy for success, decreased effort, attributions to external and uncontrollable causes, and reduced satisfaction. These ultimately translate into dissatisfaction with the educational experience, as evidenced by reduced ratings of teachers and courses.

Finally, the research of Pascarella and Terenzini (1991) summarizes changes in students in four areas: cognitive, attitudinal, psychosocial, and moral development. Included among the factors considered in these areas are communications and reasoning skills, the ability to deal with conceptual complexity, the values placed on intrinsic and extrinsic rewards, altruism and liberalism, self-concept, autonomy, psychological well-being, and the use of principled reasoning. A review of Table 10.1 shows how closely the motivational factors discussed in this volume relate to student development, not only from a cognitive perspective, but also from a broader developmental view. If in the college or university environment there is attention to the teaching, learning, and organizational motivational principles outlined in the matrix, there should be opportunities for development not only in the classroom but also through the processes and models used by the institution. Faculty who perceive a positive climate for teaching and learning (a "supportive teaching culture," to use Feldman and Paulsen's definition) will be more inclined to take part in the life of the institutional community, thus fostering inclusion for students and an enthusiastic awareness of the values of the institution and the intrinsic rewards that are part of a complete college or university experience. Being a part of this community will enhance the relevance and meaning of the work done not only by students and faculty but also by all members of the institutional community. Ultimately, the institutional mission and direction will be consistent with its day-to-day practice, leading to the kind of institutional environment suggested by Nuhfer's and Farmer's chapters in this volume: an environment in which clarity of focus and consistency in practice allow all members to participate in and contribute to institutional growth through the personal and professional growth nurtured by the institution itself.

Conclusions

There is a great deal of consistency in contemporary writing about motivation. This volume has focused on motivation for teaching, learning, and institutional programs. We have seen the models and the research of the nine contributing authors as well as the work of four others. We have considered the work of writers from other fields of inquiry. What has emerged is a consistent pattern of emphasis on a group of six factors: inclusion, attitude, meaning, competence, leadership, and satisfaction. Table 10.2 presents a reduced version of Table 10.1, extracting these six key terms.

Most of the cells in Table 10.2 are filled with an uppercase X. This indicates that the term was directly used by the authors or that it closely matches terms used in their chapters. The cells that contain a lowercase x indicate that with only minor elaboration a connection to the matrix term can be demonstrated. For example, consider the Feldman and Paulsen chapter on a

Table 10.2. Key Motivation Terms: Author by Factor Matrix

Author Factor	Wlodkowski	Paulsen[a]	Donald	Keller	MacKinnon	Panitz	Feldman[b]	Nuhfer	Farmer	Theall[c]	Pintrich	Forsyth[d]	Chickering[e]
Inclusion	X	X	X	x	X	X	X	X	X	X		X	X
Attitude	X	X	X	X	x	X	x	X	x	X	X	x	X
Meaning	X	X	X	X	X	x	x	x	x	X	X	X	X
Competence	X	X	X	X	X	X	X	x	x	X	x	X	x
Leadership	x	x	X	x	x	x	X	X	X	x		X	X
Satisfaction	x	x	x	X	x	X	x	x	X		x	X	x

[a] Paulsen and Feldman (Chapter Two).

[b] Feldman and Paulsen (Chapter Seven).

[c] Theall, Birdsall, and Franklin, 1997.

[d] Forsyth and McMillan, 1991.

[e] Chickering and Gamson, 1987.

supportive teaching culture. Only two cells of the matrix are marked with an uppercase X. This is because the eight characteristics directly outlined by the authors fit neatly into the inclusion and leadership categories. One can safely assume that if the supportive teaching culture described by Feldman and Paulsen were present at an institution, there would also be faculty awareness, interest, and enthusiasm. Likewise, the provision of faculty support mechanisms would result in an increased perception of the value of the culture and the teaching it supported. The presence of teaching centers, faculty development efforts, supportive department chairs, and other mechanisms for development could influence the quality of teaching in positive ways and lead to increased competence, the expectancy for more success, and feelings of empowerment. Given these positive outcomes, satisfaction would be almost certain to result. The same synergistic sequence can be posited without difficulty in each case. Two cells are empty in the Pintrich column only because the focus was on the MSLQ, which is quite specific in the constructs it addresses.

One interesting note is that the works that deal with programmatic or institutional perspectives (Feldman and Paulsen; Nuhfer; Farmer; Chickering and Gamson) all directly include leadership factors. Top-level participation and support of improvement efforts is a hallmark of successful programs. Even the works that focus more on motivation and learners (Donald; Theall, Birdsall, and Franklin; Forsyth and McMillan) include leadership characteristics because they incorporate the notion of the instructor as an instructional leader.

The breadth of literature in higher education provides an array of powerful tools that can be used within this motivational model. Consider how the use of Grasha's (1996) treatment of individual differences and teaching and learning styles might promote inclusion and ownership, or how Diamond's (1989) process for designing courses and curricula provides faculty with opportunities to incorporate motivational process into everyday teaching and learning. Contributing, too, are discussions of curricular issues (Gaff, 1991) or classroom research and assessment (Angelo and Cross, 1993) or the processes of successful instructional support and consultation (Brinko and Menges, 1997).

The consistency of the models clearly suggests that inclusion in a coherent community can raise awareness and enhance positive attitudes, that these benefits can bring meaning and value to academic and workplace situations, that the effort expended by those who perceive meaning will result in greater success and heightened levels of competence and confidence, and that a great deal of intrinsic satisfaction will result. This will not happen without progressive leadership, not only by those vested with titles and rank but also by all participants in a community effort directed at growth, improvement, and excellence.

Note

1. In more recent work, Pintrich (1995) discusses self-regulated learning, noting that students may regulate three dimensions of their learning: behavior, motivation/affect, and cognition. Pintrich further states that there are three components of self-regulated learning that function in relation to these dimensions, saying that students must (1) attempt to con-

trol the dimensions, (2) establish goals, and (3) accept responsibility for taking control (p. 5). Though this work is newer than Pintrich's studies with the MSLQ, it nonetheless draws on work with that instrument and the MSLQ factors more closely match terms in the matrices in Tables 10.1 and 10.2. For that reason, the MSLQ is the focus of the discussion in this chapter.

References

Angelo, T. A., and Cross, K. P. *Classroom Assessment Techniques.* (2nd ed.) San Francisco: Jossey-Bass, 1993.

Bloom, B. S., Englehart, M. D., Furst, E. J., Hill, W. H., and Krathwohl, D. R. *Taxonomy of Educational Objectives. Handbook I: the Cognitive Domain.* New York: McKay, 1956.

Brinko, K. T., and Menges, R. J. *Practically Speaking: A Sourcebook for Instructional Consultants in Higher Education.* Stillwater, Okla.: New Forums Press, 1997.

Cashin, W. E. "Do Students Rate Different Academic Fields Differently?" In M. Theall and J. Franklin (eds.), *Student Ratings of Instruction: Issues for Improving Practice.* New Directions for Teaching and Learning, no. 43. San Francisco: Jossey-Bass, 1990.

Chickering, A. W., and Gamson, Z. F. "Seven Principles for Good Practice in Undergraduate Education." *AAHE Bulletin,* 1987, *39* (7), 1987.

Diamond, R. M. *Designing and Improving Courses and Curricula in Higher Education.* San Francisco: Jossey-Bass, 1989.

Dweck, C. S. "The Role of Expectations and Attributions in the Alleviation of Learned Helplessness." *Journal of Personality and Social Psychology,* 1975, *31,* 674–685.

Forsyth, D. R., and McMillan, J. H. "Practical Proposals for Motivating Students." In R. J. Menges and M. D. Svinicki (eds.), *College Teaching: From Theory to Practice.* New Directions for Teaching and Learning, no. 45. San Francisco: Jossey-Bass, 1991.

Franklin, J. L., and Theall, M. "Disciplinary Differences, Instructional Goals and Activities, Measures of Student Performance, and Student Ratings of Instruction." Paper presented at the 73rd annual meeting of the American Educational Research Association, San Francisco, Apr. 22, 1992.

Franklin, J. L., and Theall, M. "The Relationship of Disciplinary Differences and the Value of Class Preparation Time to Student Ratings of Teaching." In N. Hativa and M. Marincovich (eds.), *Disciplinary Differences in Teaching and Learning: Implications for Practice.* New Directions for Teaching and Learning, no. 64. San Francisco: Jossey-Bass, 1995.

Gaff, J. G. *New Life for the College Curriculum: Assessing Achievements and Furthering Progress in the Reform of General Education.* San Francisco: Jossey-Bass, 1991.

Gillmore, G. "The Effects of Course Demands and Grading Leniency on Student Ratings of Instruction." Paper presented at the 75th annual meeting of the American Educational Research Association, Atlanta, Apr. 7, 1994.

Grasha, A. F. *Teaching with Style.* Pittsburgh, Pa.: Alliance, 1996.

Holland, J. L. *Making Vocational Choices.* (2nd ed.) Englewood Cliffs, N.J.: Prentice Hall, 1985.

Pascarella, E. T., and Terenzini, P. T. *How College Affects Students: Findings and Insights from Twenty Years of Research.* San Francisco: Jossey-Bass, 1991.

Perry, R. P. "Perceived Control in College Students: Implications for Instruction in Higher Education." In J. C. Smart (ed.), *Higher Education: Handbook of Theory and Research.* Vol. 7. New York: Agathon, 1991.

Pintrich, P. R. "The Dynamic Interplay of Student Motivation and Cognition in the College Classroom." In M. Maehr and C. Ames (eds.), *Advances in Motivation and Achievement: Motivation-Enhancing Environments.* Vol. 6. Greenwich, Conn.: JAI Press, 1989.

Pintrich, P. R. (ed.). *Understanding Self-Regulated Learning.* New Directions for Teaching and Learning, no. 63. San Francisco: Jossey-Bass, 1995.

Pintrich, P. R., McKeachie, W. J., Smith, D.A.F., Doljanac, R., Lin, Y., Naveh-Benjamin, M.,

Crooks, T., and Karabenick, S. "Motivated Strategies for Learning Questionnaire." (Rev. ed.) Ann Arbor, Mich.: National Center for Research to Improve Postsecondary Teaching and Learning, University of Michigan, 1988.

Smart, J. C., and Feldman, K. A. "Accentuation Effects of Dissimilar Academic Departments: An Application and Exploration of Holland's Theory." *Research in Higher Education,* 1998, *39* (4), 385–418.

Theall, M., Birdsall, M., and Franklin, J. L. "Motivating Students: A Practical Guide for Teachers." Unpublished monograph available in draft form at <http://www.uis.edu/~ctl /motive.html>, 1997.

Weiner, B. *An Attributional Theory of Motivation and Emotion.* New York: Springer-Verlag, 1986.

MICHAEL THEALL is associate professor of educational administration and director of the Center for Teaching and Learning at the University of Illinois at Springfield.

JENNIFER FRANKLIN is director of the Office of Instructional Assessment and Evaluation at the University of Arizona.

INDEX

Administration: interdisciplinary program support from, 84–85; for supportive teaching culture, 71–72
Affect, 19, 101
Aitken, N. D., 72, 73
Ambrose, S. A., 73
American Psychological Association, Task Force on Psychology in Education, 10
Ames, C., 53, 54, 55, 81
Amundsen, C., 76
Anderson, E., 76
Anderson, R. C., 22
Angelo, T. A., 76, 107
ARCS instructional motivation model, 2; computer-based instruction applications of, 40–43; description of, 39; distance learning applications of, 43–46
Armour, R. A., 72, 74
Aronson, E., 62
Assessment: of student learning in learning-centered culture, 88–89; by students, as source of feedback for faculty, 75–76
Astin, A. W., 28, 64
Astleitner, J., 40, 43
Attention, in ARCS instructional motivation model, 39, 41, 44–45
Attitude, 101, 106; developed with cooperative learning, 59–62; in Motivational Framework for Culturally Responsive Teaching, 11, 13, 14
Austin, A. E., 72, 73, 74, 75

Baird, J., 64
Bajaj, A., 22
Baldwin, R. G., 73, 75
Bandura, A., 18, 53, 55
Barrows, H. S., 49, 50, 54, 55
Bean, J., 62
Beers, S. E., 22–23
Belenky, M. F., 19
Benjamin, M., 19
Bess, J. L., 74
Beyer, K. D., 75
Biggs, J. B., 28, 29, 30, 31, 51
Biglan, A., 30
Birdsall, M., 100, 107
Black, J. B., 63
Blaney, N., 62

Bligh, D. A., 63
Bloom, B. S., 104
Bowen, H. R., 71
Boyer, E. L., 72
Boyle, R. A., 28
Brinko, K. T., 75, 107
Brookfield, S. D., 76
Brown, D., 28
Bruning, R. H., 17
Burkman, E., 40
Bush Foundation Faculty Development Project, 72

Calvert, C., 22
Cameron, J., 10
Cashin, W. E., 27, 29, 104
Change: leadership for, 90, 92, 94; motivating faculty for, 90–95; sustaining, 89–90; trust as necessity before, 89
Chavajay, P., 7
Chickering, A. W., 82, 100, 101, 102, 106, 107
Child, D., 31
Clark, B. R., 71
Clinchy, B. M., 19
Cohen, B. P., 61
Cohen, E. G., 61
Cohen, S., 61
Colbeck, C., 73, 74
Communication skills, cooperative learning's development of, 63
Community, 101, 103; cooperative learning's promotion of, 61–62; for problem-based learning, 52–54
Competence, 101, 106; cooperative learning's development of, 62–63; in Motivational Framework for Culturally Responsive Teaching, 11, 13, 14
Computer-based instruction (CBI), ARCS instructional motivation model applied to, 40–43
Confidence, 101; in ARCS instructional motivation model, 39, 41, 44–45
Consultants, as source of feedback for faculty, 75
Context: intrinsically motivating, 81; motivation for higher-order learning and, 28–29. See also Culture

Back Issue/Subscription Order Form

Copy or detach and send to:
Jossey-Bass Inc., Publishers, 350 Sansome Street, San Francisco CA 94104-1342

Call or fax toll free!
Phone 888-378-2537 6AM-5PM PST; Fax 800-605-2665

Back issues   Please send me the following issues at $23 each:
(Important: please include series initials and issue number, such as TL90)

1. TL _____

_____

_____

$ _____ Total for single issues

$ _____ Shipping charges (for single issues *only;* subscriptions are exempt from shipping charges): Up to $30, add $5^{50} • $30^{01}–$50, add $6^{50} $50^{01}–$75, add $7^{50} • $75^{01}–$100, add 9 • $100^{01}–$150, add $10 Over $150, call for shipping charge

Subscriptions   Please ❑ start   ❑ renew my subscription to *New Directions for Teaching and Learning* for the year 1999 at the following rate:

❑ Individual $56   ❑ Institutional $99
NOTE: Subscriptions are quarterly, and are for the calendar year only. Subscriptions begin with the spring issue of the year indicated above. For shipping outside the U.S., please add $25.

$ _____ Total single issues and subscriptions (CA, IN, NJ, NY and DC residents, add sales tax for single issues. NY and DC residents must include shipping charges when calculating sales tax. NY and Canadian residents only, add sales tax for subscriptions.)

❑ Payment enclosed (U.S. check or money order only)
❑ VISA, MC, AmEx, Discover Card #_____ Exp. date_____

Signature _____ Day phone _____
❑ Bill me (U.S. institutional orders only. Purchase order required.)
Purchase order #_____

Name _____
Address _____

_____

_____

Phone_____ E-mail _____

For more information about Jossey-Bass Publishers, visit our Web site at:
www.josseybass.com   **PRIORITY CODE = ND1**